W9-DCB-838

Connecting Souls

Finnish Voices in North America

An Anthology of Finnish American and Finnish Canadian Writings

Edited by

Varpu Lindström and Börje Vähämäki

ASPASIA BOOKS
Beaverton, Ontario
Canada

Other Aspasia Books publications:

Börje Vähämäki: *Mastering Finnish* (text book & cassettes), 1999
Laila Hietamies: *Red Moon over White Sea* (novel) 2000
Varpu Lindström: *From Heroes to Enemies – Finns in Canada 1937-47*, 2000
Alfons Kukkonen: *The Knights and Ladies of the Kaleva – A History*, 2000

Cover design by Martin Best from painting
by Canadian artist Helen Lucas ©

This anthology has received generous support
from NOKIA USA and NOKIA Canada.

© Each contributing author

Aspasia Books Publishing
R.R. 1
Beaverton, Ontario
Canada L0K 1A0

Printed by University of Toronto Press

Toronto, Canada, 2000

ISBN 0-9685881-2-3

CONTENTS:

PART THREE: *Connecting with Memories and the Self*

PART FIVE: *Connecting with Finnish Literature*

Introduction:

What is the Connection?

There is an abundance of talent and creativity among the Finnish communities in the United States and Canada. Many poets and writers live and work in relative isolation from peers and readers. What connects them is their Finnish cultural heritage, their ancestry, and their very isolation.

The historical event of Finnfest USA the Canadian Finnish Grand Festival coming together for the first time for Finn Grand Fest 2000 in Toronto, July 13-16, 2000 has inspired much creative and intellectual activity. The conceptualization and timing of this volume should also be credited to FGF2000. The contributors to the volume were also invited to a symposium entitled, like the book itself, "Connecting Souls – Finnish Voices in North America" which was held as a pre-festival gathering at the University of Toronto in conjunction with its Finnish Studies Program on July 12, 2000.

Most of the contributors to the anthology *Connecting Souls – Finnish Voices in North America* are previously published poets and writers. Many were contributors to a predecessor to this volume, Michael Karni's and Aili Jarvenpa's *Sampo – The Magic Mill* (1989), a volume which created a web of connections between the literary talents on this continent with a dimension of Finnishness.

While each poet and author is idiosyncratic and unique, certain shared themes, moods, and tones become discernible the more one reads these contributions. It may even be possible to detect a Finnish mythology fuelling many of our writers' imagination. The *Kalevala* is invoked in numerous pieces, some seem to have grown literally out of the world of the *Kalevala*. Other prominent themes are loneliness, political engagement, violence, and attachment to place, and to nature are prominent.

There is clearly a sense in many poems or stories that the connection to Finnish culture operates on at least two time levels. The level of the cultural heritage which has been passed on by parents, grandparents or great grandparents is very strong indeed. However, increasingly there is also a personal (re)discovery of contemporary Finnish culture acquired through travel to, and often lengthy stays in, Finland. The triangle of past Finnish cultural heritage, familiarity with present Finland-

Finnish culture, and the self yields a sense of wholeness and insightfulness which feeds creativity.

Out of the multitude and rich variety of the contributed texts, this book has been organized into five parts. The first part consists of poems and stories which deal more or less overtly with the *Kalevala*, or a special relationship with nature. Both of these phenomena owe much to the shamanistic world view of Finns and Finno-Ugrians. The second part focuses on the immigrant experience, on being Finnish in North America and all that may entail. Some of those experiences are heart-wrenching, others humorous, all perceptive and interesting.

Part three, while being the most indistinct, is also the largest. The question of identity, which is integral also to the texts in parts one and two, becomes central, and clearly more subjective in this section. Memory is the most important prerequisite for the continuity of identity; the self is a construct pieced together by memory and with memories.

The experience of visiting Finland or living in Finland for a while can often be decisive in a person's life. Part four, therefore, is called (Re)Connecting with Finland, and consists of texts which give expression to the consequences such visits have had for the individual. It also includes stories of non-Finnish Americans who typically have lived in Finland, had memorable experiences, and observed "Finnishness in action." They write "Finnish voices" as well.

A considerable portion of the book is devoted to translation of Finnish poetry and short stories. This is one way the triangle can be formed between Finnish heritage in North America, modern Finnish culture, and the self. As has been the case throughout history, many poets and writers are also translators, so too in this volume. *Connecting Souls - Finnish Voices in North America* illustrates the great connections which exist, between continents, between generations, between people, between souls.

Varpu Lindström and Börje Vähämäki

PART ONE:

Connecting with Finnish Mythology and Nature

Harry Gustafsson

Kullervo

For a suffering soul,
suicide,
is the gift of
life.

Childhood memories broken,
I'm sinking,
deeper into
the smithy's heat,
my life annihilated,
in a
tearing fire.

As we dwell,
search,
the enigma continues,
Väinämöinen
Ilmarinen
Lemminkäinen,
the gods
of our forefathers
will always be
steeped in mystery.
We have a key,
where is the lock?

In life
I held her hand,
In death
she holds mine,
life and death,
a bubbling brook
from eternity
on Kalevala's heath.

Ilmatar,
genesis of Kalevala,
alumni,
the human spirit.

I laid my head
on Kantele's musical down,
to slumber peacefully
in childhood bliss
from the cares
of this earth
after a day
well spent
on Kalevala's heath,
its musings
I tried to understand.

Through the clouds
gnarled and bony
hands of the moon
gripped the hearts
of the people
on Kalevala's heath,
a sign in the sky
of impending doom,
Kullervo's curse
had begun.

In my mind
there is always
a thought
that beckons beyond,
could it be
my origins
on Kalevala's heath
trying to get through?

When my sister died
I was envious
of the beautiful coffin,
made on Kalevala's heath.

As the stars fell
the mist rose,
her life ended
at the beginning.

Burt Rairamo

THE SEARCH

As sage Väinämöinen
I drifted down the empty spaces,
swam the oceans' far horizons,
searching----

After ages I spotted land,
the island of life's oasis.
-----it faded into haze.

I kept on searching,
listening to my inner callings,
following a faintly beacon,
echoing a distant past.

Then I saw a foggy island,
the island of man's hopes.
----it vanished in a fog.

I drifted deeper, always farther
in the dark and endless waters
at the edges of the vast expanses
----searching

At last I reached a rocky shore,
the island of one's dreams,
---as Atlantis,
it sank beneath my feet.

Still I drift and search
the empty spaces,
swim the oceans' far horizons.
I lift my eyes and pray to Ukko,
the mighty thunder G-d of sky.

Jane Piirto

*"He was there as second man: / with butter
he smeared the locks / the hinges with fat."*   **Runo 42**

FOR THE CLUBBERS

a row of lilacs in bloom
beside every house
the lilac air odorous
scent of damp spring earth
small hushed peace of homecoming
descends as through the covered copse
wall and tree, a rustle of wind
verdant essence flows gentle
sway of mountain ash resounds

my Finnish heart, green meadows
woods, pines, birches, birds in trees
in fields they teeter on reeds
this long bright green swath fenced in
stern gray ghostly granite posts
footprints in pine-needle sand
native crows silhouetted
on faraway branches

Outi, *Kalevala* teacher
sits on a wall, her feet splayed
sings us the Bothnian song
looks off into fair spring air in
translation concentration:

Vaasan Marssi

we were born and we grew up
in the wide and open lands
of Bothnia where the seas
and the rivers flow
billows of the green blue sea
we grew up with land cold like its trees

we can't be frightened by the weather
and even the winters can't kill us
nor does poverty and misery
of the flat woodland and the wasteland

here we are, four hundred years
later, at this coffin-like
monument with its bronze plaque
Nvijamiehille 1597 ("For the Clubbers")
peasant uprising against
the Swedish rulers

they tell us
we are kin of the rebel,
the peasant leader,
Jakob Ilkka, who
fought on this hill near
our lilac-scented family farm
our ancestral fathers' land
here

our father's father Herman
oldest son, why did he emigrate?
probably sat, June, 1900
before he left this home ground
for damp, cold, underground, iron mines
on the Marquette Range in Michigan
where he would die of skin rot
where his wife's brother would die
of a falling chunk, only three weeks after
arriving, full of hope for the new land
my land, too

The bench-sitters will not sing / if the bench-sitters do not
/ and the floors will not declare / if the floor-treaders do not" **Runo 21**

TANGO FINLAND

the outdoor pavilion Katamu Lava
at 10 p.m. sun blaze in June midsummer
famous tango singer Eino Grön
gives a concert at the dance

single women line up on a bench along the wall
flowered dresses leather pumps
purses with long string thin straps
slung across their round bosoms

single men in open throat print shirts
polyester or part-cotton pants
thin black socks, black leather shoes
rush over to the women

ask them for dancing
sweat blends with perfume
beer and mosquitoes
folk whirl like dervishes

II.
Last week at the university
my student Sini wrote an essay
Why do Finns love the tango? I asked.

> *"The tango is considered a very emotional dance. However, we*
> *Finns are often thought to be people who don't want to show*
> *their feelings easily. Why do we still love to dance and sing*
> *tango? What's the secret in tango? Why do we love it so much*
> *and think it is almost more Finnish than Argentinean?*
>
> *I think this is all due to our character. We, especially our men,*
> *are usually very shy. They don't laugh a lot, they don't cry, they*
> *don't know how to express their feelings to the opposite sex.*
> *But they can dance beautifully. They can tango, they can make*
> *lyrics, and they can sing.*
>
> *The lyrics of tangos are strong and emotional. If they are written*
> *by other Finns, we can understand the meaning because they tell*
> *about feelings we all experience. In fact, by dancing, singing, and*

18

*listening to tangos, we have found a way to show our deepest
feelings.*

*There is fire in the Argentine tango; we have longing and yearn-
ing in ours. We both tell about love.*

so. blood tells.
so this is why I wanted to dance tango
all night, that month in Argentina

a red-faced man comes over
asks me to the dance
we hop all over the floor
a polka, not a tango

he speaks only Finnish
I English
my black Nikes don't glide well
his breath smells stale beer

my cousin circles the side, teasing
with a camera to capture
my Finnish *poika* polka
my drunk Finnish swain

he says "I love you"
his only English
I giggle
lead him back to the bench

Eino is singing
like a lounge singer
in Fort Lauderdale
where he spends winters
gold chains adorn his broad neck
his Hawaiian shirt

oh Sini
the accordion is not the bandoneon
the polka is not tango
no one asks me to tango
they think I am an alien
in my black Nikes from the U.S.
the crowd gathers round Eino
with applause! applause! Applause!

Ted Jansen

MY FINNISH HERITAGE AND THE *KALEVALA* – A MEMOIR

When I started the study of the *Kalevala* in the Department of Finnish Studies three years ago, I did not know what alliteration was, let alone a trochaic tetrameter. Neither poetry nor mythology had ever been part of my education as a mechanical engineer. Searching for my Finnish roots and wanting to examine my Finnish identity, I found the Finnish Studies program at the University of Toronto, and the *Kalevala* world. Elias Lönnrot's 1849 poem is a myth, the effects of which in the "real" world are very wide-ranging. But I had no inkling, on that cold January afternoon, of just how many ways in which it would enrich my life.

The study of the *Kalevala* first of all improved my understanding of my Finnish heritage. My mother was born in Karelia, in Nunnanlahti, near Juuka. Her stories of her childhood and her life there as a young woman were moving, poignant, and they reverberated in the *Kalevala*. She loved to ski and she would tell how, as a youngster, she skied the ten kilometres to school, through the forest. Until she was older the distance was too great for her to come home each day; as a child she could only come home on the weekends. How she missed her parents! In 1914 the food supplies from Russia stopped and there was widespread hunger in Karelia. My mother often told of eating birch bark in order to stay alive. She would 'Gnaw the famine bread of pine bark' (Runo 33, l.34). (It is interesting that a research institute in Kuopio is currently investigating the effects of adding small amounts of tree bark to cereals fed to humans.) My mother told of how, as a girl, she was courted by an older man. She refused his attention. It was

> 'Better a fish among the fishes
> Than to be an old man's comfort
> And a refuge to a trembler,
> Tottering around in stockinged feet' (Runo 4, l. 247-53)

As a young woman she worked on a farm, looking after the cattle, sometimes staying up all night to help with the birth of animals. For all

20

the work she was only paid with one pair of shoes, per year, and this more than anything else made her decide to emigrate. She left for Canada in 1928 at the age of twenty-four with thousands of other young single Finnish women. Her father accompanied her to the train station in Joensuu. To more firmly secure her suitcase he took the belt from his trousers. This kind gesture so affected her that she almost decided to stay. 'You are going for a long time/ Forever from your father's shelter' (Runo 22, I. 117-8). She was a very determined woman: once she had made up her mind, there was no moving her from her position. Like a ship at anchor, she would firmly hold on to her goal, regardless how rough the seas. When she was just married, she lived for sometime with her in-laws. 'The Teaching of the Bride' (Runo 23) is a fitting image of this period in her life, a period of difficult personal adjustments.

The *Kalevala* made me listen to music in a new way. Last New Year's Eve the Canadian Broadcasting Corporation presented on television an elaborate overview of the celebrations, in the form of music and dance, around the world. The most outstanding performance was, in my view, the presentation of 'Luonnotar' at Tampere Hall. 'Luonnotar', a miniature concerto by Sibelius for solo voice and orchestra, is based on Runo 1 of the *Kalevala* which deals with the birth of the universe, the Finnish story of Creation.

'Olipa impi, ilman tytto, ...'

'There was a maiden, daughter of the heavens,
the beautiful Luonnotar,
who pondered on the meaning of her life,
a life spent all alone
in the vast emptyness of space.'

Sibelius used the *Kalevala* for much of his work. The earliest *Kalevala*-inspired composition was 'Kullervo', performed by the Toronto Symphony Orchestra in June of 1997 as part of the Northern Encounters Festival. The third and fifth movements use solo voices and chorus to narrate the tragic tale of Kullervo's seduction of his sister and his suicide. Kullervo, 'Eternal Drifter, ever moving/Shelterless beneath the sky' (Runo 34, I. 47-48). In 'Lemminkäinen in Tuonela', based on Runos 14 and 15, the initial tone is ominous with the theme (typically) repeated three times as Lemminkäinen, searching for the swan, is destined to be killed by Pohjola's cowherd. The music then takes on a magical, shamanistic, quality as the incantations by Lemminkäinen's

21

mother put her son back together: 'Though her magic healed the veins/ Neatly knit the veins together' (Runo 15, l.381-2).

The *Kalevala* poetry inspired me to read other poets: Rilke, T.S. Eliot and Baudelaire; its rhythm and sounds have given me a new appreciation for the acoustics in my own profession. The rhythm of the *Kalevala* in the Friberg translation is filled with what I can only describe as a sensuousness that I have heard and felt in the droning of a low speed Diesel engine! That magical machine, the Sampo, inspired me to write the following as a comment on our quest for ever more efficient machines:

'Ever, output over input,
Sacred ratio of the trade
Must forever be increasing,
Searching for the demon Chaos:
Irreversibilities!
Second Law is never broken,
Clausius' Inequality'.

In early December I heard again the voices from the *Kalevala* when the chamber choir Vox Finlandiae and the Fireside Epic storytellers presented the 'Sounds of *Kalevala*' at the Agricola Finnish Lutheran Church. I heard again the sounds of Karelia. In the magical atmosphere of the church my mother's stories of Karelia, told long ago, mingled with the 'Sounds of *Kalevala*'. I greatly appreciate the course 'Finnish Folklore: the *Kalevala*' at the University of Toronto; it was instrumental in giving depth and colour to my Finnish cultural heritage.

Diane Jarvenpa

WHERE THERE IS SINGING

It all turns quiet
in this home of women fading to closure,
the angel-beauty growing
tired. It has come to this,
to these women, a cloudbank of widows
murmuring to themselves of old storms.
This is your family now
with whom you take your communion,
sing the hymns of the body spent.

I ask you to sing
in this room
with its buzzer and pull cord,
life lines you cannot reach.
You and I sing together.
Today the words ascend scales, climb high
where a swirl of notes gets deposited
and left abruptly. Two languages
settle in the air like steam
nurtured from stone.

I place the books you have written into
your hands. You hold them with a sweet
separateness with which one would hold the idea
of winter never having known snow.

I read you your words,
I sing the other language.
You fix your gaze to place and time,
pull back, pull in,
fumbling in the dark.
What you want to forget
finally comes to you,

absence crowded with imperfection,
that old tongue.

Today while they are bathing you
I sit as you did, read the old runes.

It is this that links us,
an old poem voiced in despair
and gratitude, bringing me closer
to your childhood's silent days,
the immigrant suffering, thinning your bones.

Matalana maammostani
jäin kuin kiuruksi kivelle,
rastahaksi rauniolle,
kiuruna kivertämähän,
on mua kuuset kuulemassa,
hongan oksat oppimassa,
koivun lehvät lempimässä,
pihlajat pitelemässä.

Today you shook loose a long low song,
with bended notes,
a floating picture I climbed into
as I would a boat pushed from a dock
like the many boats we kids rocked in,
canoes we carried, pulled on sand,
paddled eagerly away,
you on shore smiling, waving,
growing smaller,
among trees and sky,
you, just a fleck of white,
then gone.

(italics: from *The Kalevala*)
(I have been without a mother
Like a lark on stone abandoned
Like a small thrush on a cairn
Left to sing there as a lark bird.
- Only fir trees listen to me
Only pine boughs left to teach me
Tenderness I get from birch leaves
And caresses from the rowan.)

IN THE DEEP WOODS

This is where your grandmother
came to pick mushrooms
in her new country,
belly empty, mind scattered,
mud and tears slick on her boots.
Here in the deep woods
she came to loosen pain,
break it off of its wheel,
let it drop off her skin
with the old rotting trunks of aspen.

She walked under thunderheads,
around bramble fires and the thumbprints
of early floods, the whirlpooling eddies
and foam soaking her skirts.
After the drowning white of winter,
she came to find carpets of twinflowers
spreading across snow-soaked hills,
the whole world stretching
and birthing newness.

Here she tasted liquor on her lips
of wintergreen and red raspberry,
sap of sugar maples,
the sweet and the bitter
flowing inside her,
filling the vacuum of regret.

This is where she came
stepping quietly into the deep woods,
thorns gripping, mayflies billowing,
sitting alone on that old stump
at the center of the New World,
spellbound by its strange, imperfect land.
Watching the delicate nests
of the many small birds,
understanding their sudden,
brilliant flash of wings.

TUNDRA SWANS

They feed on the wild celery,
a symposium of white wings
folding and unfolding old stories
while the snow is still nothing but seeds
banked in skies weeks away.
What makes us stand here like children
listening to them as if they were telling us
some fable we desperately needed to hear?

Winking and disappearing inside the reeds,
they spin the fairy tale over and over
of persecution and resurrection,
the slippered girl in the silver tutu
pointing out that thin blue line
where life can cross back over on itself
and each season high spirals into the next.

Like a cloudburst set low between the hills
their many sudden shades of pearl,
cotton bloom, lily bulb and ice floe
beat feet upon the water and go up
as if that was what water was for
to launch yourself element to element.
Hundreds of swans leaving the tundra behind
burying their heads inside their wings
to sleep the curled sleep of snakes and cats
and all those classical O's of nature that dazzle us
like dogs sleepless under a full moon.
Here in the steady surf of wings
shimmering in their finer orbits,
their black beaks drink it in,
drink at the great dark bowl of earth,
the same earth that shrinks at our touch
and swells to hold seas for their feasting.
And you and I standing here
watching the surface of the lake,
stunned by bird and sky,
thirsty for them.

Paula Erkkila

SONG OF A NEW *SAMPO*

Heroes and heroines
Arise from the archipelago
Bring back the copper boats
Pick up the rocks
Oh sons and daughters
Of Kaleva and Pohjola
Let us forge a new *sampo*
Shine new sun and gleam new moon
Let us fill the air with joy
Ilmatar grant us rebirth
Wake up Vipunen's Antero
Sing of our ancient Uralic magic

Sail back to the fatherland
Climb the rocks of Hanko
Embrace the grandmothers and grandfathers
Listen for their stories
Finish the songs still fresh on their lips
Put on the *huivis* and *lakkis* of wisdom
And let your passions flow
Bring out the *vihtas*, the cedar and the birch
Heat up the sauna once again
Bring back the old *kuppari* woman
And heal our many wounds
Let us hear the *noitas* chant and hum

27

Look into the archipelago of your mind
Join the old and steadfast Väinämöinen
On his rocky isle of pine
Hold hands with the heroes
Ilmarinen and Lemminkäinen
Louhi's daughter break the spell of the seagull
Kyllikki come back and defend your honor
Sing a song duel with Joukahainen proud and strong

Kullervo let go of revenge and find your peace
Aino face the man and tell him no
Rise from the sea and breathe new life
Oh gods and goddesses of land air and water
Out with the *potkukelkkas*
Onto the snows of Pohjola
Louhi get out your nine stallions
Share our *sampo* and reclaim our power
Find the old magic drums with the old brass rings
And search for the reindeer once again
Search for those things we have lost
Collect the scattered pieces of ourselves
Oh mother of Lemminkäinen
Take a spirit journey to Tuonela's land of the dead
Fly to the farthest reaches of the heavens
Fly to the farthest reaches of the heavens
Find those honey bees with the nectar of life's souls

Celebrate this glorious resurrection
Let the cuckoos sing and sing
Let the wedding begin
Weep for a happier marriage
Prepare for the guests
Bring in the *nisua* woman, the singers, and the storytellers
Out with the *kanteles* with those sweet and birdlike trills
Throw the knives onto the rafters
Make way for Anssi's Jukka to fight a worthy fight
Invite the old poppas and seers
Chant the old snake charms
Let the *loitsiminen* begin

Let us forge a new *sampo*
With our grandparents and grandchildren
With Jumala and Ilmatar
With our gods and goddesses and spirits of the earth
Antero release the magic words and charms
Rise up Ural of our blood
Out of the woods you bears of Perm
Flow Volga through our veins
March forward you knights and ladies of Pori and Tallinn
Heroes and heroines
Of Kaleva and Pohjola
Arise to new glory.

Susan Vickberg-Friend

AUTOBIOGRAPHICAL STATEMENT
ABOUT MY POETRY

An odour smelt
an emotion felt
an abundant bundle of bunkl
a profound thought thunk
a deal known through touch
a feel involving much
Imagery that is found
through the joy of sound
describing crying
talking about trying
perhaps in the middle
a little riddle
and sometimes
it all rhymes.

ME AND SAMPO

My childhood imagination was all a gawk
As my grandpappa Walter narrated to me
Fantastic tales and talk
He'd brought with him from his birth country;
Anecdotes from the *Kalevala* epic story.

It was sauna evenings when we talked the most.
"I already know how Väinämöinen built his boat!"
I would proudly boast.
"Tell me about that ancient Finnish prosperity machine,
tell me some more stories of Sampo;"
I'd request, with moist sauna steam in my throat.

And that's just what Grandpappa Walter did;
he told me the myth of the fantastic Sampo machine,
its magical function, and its chimerical lid.
In modern times Sampo has never been seen;
but I learned how it was made, and where it was hid!

As the sauna steam grew hot
I wanted to hear yet again
how Sampo had been stolen –
    We would sing a short, magic song
    that put all Pohjola into a long,
    sound, deep,
    shaman's sleep.
    Keeping beat with the *vihta*,
    together we'd count
    the locks which needed to be open.
    One through nine; the last made ten.
    So, Sampo was found,
    rooted into the ground.
    Stuck, in the muck.
    It would not budge
    until given a nudge,

and a sturdy pull
by an enormous bull.
Finally,
from within Copper Mountain,
Sampo was free!
Väinämöinen stole it into his boat, then
he set sail with Sampo
into a wild, wavy, stormy sea.

Grandpappa Walter worked hard to make a living;
Sampo was always riches churning out and giving.
I was convinced I had everything that
It would take, to make
My very own Sampo,
Just as Ilmarinen had, in his blacksmith's forge
So very long ago –
I found a swan feather
and from my sweater
I snipped a thread.
From a slice of bread
I took a crumb,
and from a milk-bottle I took some.
I was sure I didn't really need a heifer!
In my palm I rolled them all,
and molded them into a perfect ball.
I waited until the sauna oven was extremely hot.
With careful aim, and my very best shot
I flipped my magic, little ball
into the sauna oven, with no doubt at all
that quite soon within the glow
I'd see a magnificent crossbow.
I threw another log into the fire
and watched the sparks jump even higher.
I was sure that before long
to the top of the flames would float
a most grand, and glorious boat.
Amongst the sparks and flames I insist I saw
a shining sun-disc, and sparkling bear-star.
I knew that within the oven, somehow
There would then appear a great cow

which would be followed by a powerful plough;
after that, Sampo would take form.
The fantastic machine would be born.

Grandpappa Walter softly said:
"Come on; -- it is time to go."
I protested, I shouted: "No-o-o-o;
I have not finished forging my own Sampo!"

That night Grandpappa Walter comforted me
as I watched the sauna oven grow cold.
In a few short years
my Grandpappa Walter grew very old.
    I think of Grandpappa Walter frequently.
    And in my heart I know:
    that should Sampo be a machine of today,
    it could not bring absolute prosperity
    but certainly,
    it would be built to be
    the foremost in technology
    of the twenty-first century.

SNOW

Snow.

Neither a purple flower,
nor a red one;
    greens gone,
    violets vanished
    spectrum swallowed.

The roadways and,
all sidewalks, too;
    details deleted,
    markings removed,
    boundaries blended.

The sun visible,
high in the sky;
    light bright,
    warmth waned,
    heat halted.

More snow.

SECOND MILLENNIUM

Y2K.

Y to K.

Why to K ?

However, not K, but to two K's.

Counting years, moving through time to double K.

"K" for "kilo;" meaning 'thousand.'

Why two K ?

In Roman numerals "thousand" is written "M."

Two thousand being stated as "MM."

If M equals thousand;

Why too, K ?

Carol Ruotsala Staats

MOON COVE

The wolf-eye tide sluices deep bedrock-run channels
past islets and inlets, long fingers of bay,
baring slag-nobbled ironstone reef hung with kelp-whip,
nestling trembling dippers of cold
molten moon.

The long silent coving of onyx arch rolling . . .
glistening broad, blunt black tail,
poised like night wings of bird,
smacks the sea as the whale sounds
and blows.

And the tapestry night woven tight, fine with starfire
banners wide with its bright discus eye.
And the fjord peaks are shimmering, shearing
cant angles upthrust coldstone spires,
cleft in two, black and white.

The wind stirs the flame in the moon-struck medallion,
thin twin-wafer mirrored on the lagoon.
Wind pleats the waves, deftly plaiting pure light
through the moss-hung spruce arrows
and gnarled alder trees.

The harsh growling cataract rumbles the echo
of boulders across the blue shadows,
across the black water into the dark hills
while the sea sifts the pebbles
in gentling cove.

STONE HARVEST

We picked a half ton or so of stones
from fields where Lapland fingerlings

had grown, their color saffron
like the Arctic fells in autumn.

I harvested two artifacts
whose heft and fit in hand

convinced me
of their true identity,

though not in situ,
and a seasoned twisted root.

The diamond latticework
of branches bare, wind tossed

against the graying sky
betokened rain, or sleet.

I finished with the morning task,
and now my ancient eye

will try to read the mystery
of the magic root and stones.

AFTERNOON GRACE

It was late afternoon in the mountains,
golden afternoon of the year,
when we stretched near the blooming azalea
in the winter-silkened straw.
You said, watching a cloud drift and change,
"I would like to discover one truth
and be happy forever. One single
unqualified, unalterable truth abiding."

And in that calm upland meadow,
sweet with bloom and gently sad grass,
anything, all things, seemed possible.
still, the flycatcher hid its trumpet
among the violets, even then,
and the wasp, burring in tune
with the deer fly, hid its sting.

How many afternoons have passed?

The juggler's fingers tire, our world wobbles.
And what would you do with that great
flaming flare on a yo-yo string?

My treasure of truth is on my head
and in it. Small change
heaped upon small change, and grace
to know that this is so
before this heap is spent.

EMBERS STIRRING

I stir the sullen ash
and blow upon the ember,
the pitch of blackened spruce
crackles, flares to flame.

I stand, transfixed, by memory
of an early fire, stare into the hope
of warmth and light against the bitter dark
and wind and chill of winter.

Our autumn canopy of gold
is falling, vanishing
like summer's spark, our innocence
has fled, our seasons pass

like childhood dreams
we only half remember,
and childhood joys
we only half forget.

OLD MAPS, OLD FACES

We follow old maps, old faces,
vellum, crinkled parchment,
finely drawn, and etched by memory,
odd longitudes and latitudes
not Mercator's stiff projections.
No glossy reprints, these,
but worn reflections,
legends in old-fashioned script
illuminating paths and voyages.
Deep lakes beside the promontory,
arroyos, dry,
in season cursed with flashing flood.
The cliffs and crags well-marked
with cross-hatched shadowings,
old caves, with hidden treasure,
these boundless Eldorados.

PART TWO:

Connecting with the New World

Lynn Maria Laitala

ASHES: JUSSI'S STORY

Many Finnish men left their families behind when they emigrated to North America — and many were never heard from again. One may well wonder what happened to those men. The Iron Range of Minnesota had the highest industrial accident rate in the world in 1910 and many unidentified immigrant miners were buried in unmarked graves. It was just as easy to lose one's life in a logging camp. But there were other reasons, too. A new woman perhaps. Or something else.

Such a strange country. Big fluffy snowflakes drifting down on a warm May morning.

No, not snowflakes. Ash.

I smelled fire.

I ran to the barn. Mrs. Järvinen was already there, slapping and cursing the cows, driving them from their stanchions. I helped little Helmi herd them outside.

"Helmi and I can bring them to Isaakson's clearing," Mrs. Järvinen yelled at me. "You stay here."

Mr. Järvinen was climbing the ladder to the roof of the barn. I passed buckets of water up to him, and he threw them on roof.

Untinen came running up the road.

"We'll try to stop the fire here. Others are coming," he shouted.

I took my place on the ladder, passing buckets of water up to the men who wet down the roof of the barn, dousing sparks that fell on the cedar shingles. Others worked furiously at the edge of the field with shovels and picks, trying to make a trench that the fire wouldn't jump.

Not our puny efforts, but the wind and rain saved the Järvinen farm. The fire took its own course. It burned the sauna that stood beyond the house, but not the barn. It came so close to the yard that the heat ignited the pile of chips under the swing I was making for little Helmi, but the log house still stood.

The fire raged through, heat singeing hair and mustaches, blistering faces. It swept through Birch Lake Township, jumped the lake and burned to the south shore of Fall Lake before the rains stopped it.

Other neighbors didn't do as well. There was no man at the Niemi place, only a woman and her half-grown boys. The boys got their cows out, but when they went home to save something else, the cows followed them back. The cows, house, barn—everything burned except the boys and their mother, and one old rooster, who came out from somewhere after the fire.

My little dog Kauhu blistered the pads of his feet, walking over the smoldering ground. I packed them in a pine tar poultice, and they healed.

Some of the homesteaders who were burned out moved away. The Sutelas left, and the Tuhkanens. I let the Järvinens find another hired man, and went to work in the logging camps on the lakes. I wanted to be near water.

There were over a hundred men in the camp on Hoist Bay. We slept in dark, vermin-infested bunkhouses in long rows, two to a bunk. Two tiny windows let in meager light. We were fed rotten food, mostly beans and tainted salt pork.

I was bitterly sorry I'd ever come to this country, so far from my beautiful wife and my darling little girls in Finland.

"Soon," I had told Irja when I left, "Soon I will send for you."

It was a miracle that she had chosen me for a husband. I couldn't believe my luck. I'm a small man, and not brave. Irja said that she liked my gentle way, but still, it was hard to understand.

After our marriage, my prospects dimmed. My father had co-signed notes for someone who didn't pay up, and we lost the farm. I sent my wife and daughters home to her family, and set out for America to make my fortune.

Every night I dreamed of Irja caressing my face, kissing the lids of my closed eyes, only to awaken to loneliness, tossing about on a lumpy straw mattress next to a foul smelling man.

Often at the camps, talk turned to women. Most of the men had left home as boys so they'd never had a real girlfriend. Now they didn't have much chance of getting one because there weren't enough girls to go around.

All they had known were whores.

"What's the matter with you, Jussi," Heikki said, one time up on Hoist Bay. "You never want a woman on payday."

44

"Don't you like women?" Arne taunted.

I didn't mean to tell them anything, but I couldn't take the jeers.

"I'm faithful to my wife. I'm going to bring her over when I get the money saved for her ticket," I said.

That made their taunts worse.

"And who would marry you? Was she ugly or was she some old hag who couldn't get another man?"

"Irja is young and beautiful," I said.

"Well then, what's the chance that she's faithful to you, runt that you are? There must be lots of big strong men left in Finland who can make a beautiful woman happy."

After that, whenever they came back to the camp, hung-over and broke, after they'd spent all their money in the bars and brothels in Winton, they would make themselves feel better by telling me what a fool I was.

"There you sit, while a man is unbuttoning Irja's dress," Heikki would say.

"Now he's putting his hand on her bare thigh," Arne went on.

Irja stopped coming to me in my dreams. Whenever I closed my eyes I was tormented by visions of her in another man's arms.

I said to myself, she's better off with him than with me. The kindest thing is for me to let her be.

I never talked about Irja anymore, but the men kept on with their mockery, until Antti came to camp.

Antti was a powerful man, over six feet tall, and strong as an ox.

"Which of us was man enough to find a wife?" Antti challenged my tormentors. "Do you think that cutting down a tree makes you a real man? Or gulping a bottle of booze in one swig?"

The others were silent. Not only was Antti a big man, he was strongest on the cross-cut, smoothest with the axe. He could handle a team—four or six horses, it made no difference—and he was a wizard at the forge.

They listened to Antti.

"None of us had what it took to win a woman's love. You're jealous of Jussi because he did. You're just like a mink that pisses on what it can't eat."

That put an end to the teasing, but not an end to my misery. In my heart I knew that the others were right. Irja could never have stayed faithful to a man like me.

Irja wrote to me for many years, but I never answered.

It was hard to forget my children. I made toys out of wood for Mrs. Rautio's daughters, and gave them nickels to buy candy wondering; how big are my little girls now? Did they call another man father?

Memory dimmed with the passing of time. I'd almost forgotten my long-ago home in Finland when Auvo Pertti came to Winton. I remembered him as a little boy in my village, listening with big ears to stories about the riches America had to offer. He had grown up and come across the ocean to get some of those riches for himself, and to look for me.

Auvo found me in my room at Rautio's boardinghouse. He gave me a letter, crumpled and soiled from travel. After he had gone, I unfolded it carefully.

> *Husband,*
> *I wait for word from you, but no word comes. I fear that you are dead, but I never give up hope that you are well, and will some day send for me. If you are alive, what terrible fate has befallen you, that keeps us apart?*
> *I remain faithfully yours,*
> *Your loving wife.*
> *Irja.*

Memories of Finland flooded back. In my mind I followed Irja there alone, the Irja I had not believed in, living through the years on fading hope. What was she doing right now?

It was haymaking time. Villagers were joining farmers in the fields, pitching mown grass on stakes to cure. Maybe the haymakers were resting, refreshing themselves with buttermilk and rye bread. Irja would be among them, and the girls. I could see them clearly, a little girl bringing her mother wild berries, the mother caressing her child's hair, bending to kiss her forehead.

I looked around at my bare room.

If only the flames that turned Irja's letter to ash could have scorched the shame from my heart.

Liisa V. Heverin-Davis

THE FAT, BLONDE, KID, AMERICAN 1926

The expectant parents of the fat, blonde kid were sure of one thing. When this kid got born, it would be 100% American kid. Having arrived from Finland quite recently they were sure that procedures must be different in here (where the streets were not really paved with gold). Feeling a need for guidance, they wrote to the United States Government for advice. Surely the Government had information regarding the feeding and care of an American kid. Everything in America was bigger and better and the Government had instructions for everything. The kid hoped they would hurry! She was tired of sitting upside down in that dark, crowded womb. It was so boring and besides, her legs got cramps. Even so, it was comforting to know that she was getting parents who knew what they were doing.

She could hardly wait for the Fourth of July, which was to be her birthday; a really great for an American kid to get born! She hoped that supper would be early that day and dishes done; no sense getting born into a messy household.

One morning while the kid was idly humming to herself and practicing toe touches, she heard someone knock at the door. Her mother hurried to open the door. At last, it was the postman bringing the booklet from the U.S. Government Printing Office; all of the information one could hope for about how to raise an American kid! She was elated; everything was sure to be O.K. now (O.K. means very good in American).

Now that her parents had official U.S. Government instructions the kid thought it a foolish waste of time to keep on sitting in there, all scrunched up until the Fourth of July!

Out in the world she could hear the birds singing and she so wanted to see the sunshine. She waited until after supper that evening and as soon as the dishes were done, she did it! Although the Fourth of July would have been the perfect birthday for an American kid, her father said that the twenty-ninth of June would be just fine. Besides, now the kid could see the fireworks with the rest of the family.

Her mother followed all of the instructions from the U.S. Government and the kid grew and thrived. She ate boiled, mashed carrots and shredded, raw apple. She drank orange juice and gnawed on chicken bones. The milkman brought her milk, always from one special cow at the dairy. He said that she could come to say hello to the cow...if she would like to, but the kid hadn't learned to walk yet.

The neighbors said: "No one feeds a kid that way, all they need for the first six months is milk." The fat, blonde kid's mother kept right on doing it anyway. After all, the U.S. Government had sent the instructions. Surely the U.S. Government knew best how to raise an American kid!

And mother was right! The kid grew to be one of the biggest, healthiest kids in all of Staten Island, New York; a genuine, 100% American kid.

Lorraine Kasari Loiselle

A CENTURY AGO

Fiina came first. The cold mouth
of Maine's winter air chewed at her
tightly buttoned coat, her head scarf,
as she took a tentative step ashore.
Finland, land of lonely farms and saunas,
endless pines and endless lakes,
where imagination named a plump red fruit
cloudberry, where sunsets dazzled,
and where Väinämöinen altered history,
slid silently into an irretrievable past.

Lovingly I try to lay in my mind
the hand-stitched clothing folded neatly
in her suitcase: woolens for warmth,
petticoats with lace for self-esteem,
a good dress. She could cook, crochet,
cut out cotton housedresses
without a pattern, and had mastered
the esoteric art of tatting.

Who met this quiet, steady-eyed woman
of twenty who spoke no English? What eager
network guided her to a job as a linotypist
on the *Raivaaja* in Fitchburg, Massachusetts,
a job she would hold for forty-four years?
She earned enough money to send
for her younger sisters and brothers:
Taimi, Lempi, Annie,
Eine, Arthur and Paavo.

My mother was her only child, as I was
my mother's only child.
I yearned to know more but no one told
stories about the old country.
No one breathed a word.
this was common.

Surely the mother and father in Pori
grieved to lose their children.
Could you bear it, to part forever
with seven beautiful and strong children?
No faded, crinkled letters exist
testifying to this unutterable loss.
Nothing for me to hold, to finger travel,
to find a way into that sealed past.

I was three months from being born
when my parents packed up a truck,
drove across Massachusetts to North Adams.
Eino had a job waiting for him:
movie theatre projectionist.
Iria had no place to land.
They drove around for hours
in their rented truck
and found finally a second floor
apartment with a wide sunny porch.
We migrated back to Fitchburg when times
got better.

When I was young, I'd visit the *Raivaaja*
after school and shyly slip past the busy
workers and the clattering machines
to my grandmother's location on the floor.
Standing all day, her job was to fit
small metal letters into huge trays.
She'd reach into a drawer
and find a velvety butterscotch for me.

Though we made do with her Finnish
and my English, no stories were told,
no memories retrieved. No words existed
to reveal the lost connections, landscape,
the heart's diary.

Jane Piirto

THE FINNISHNESS OF MY AMERICANNESS

Last Christmas Eve, at a feast at my son-in-law's parents' apartment in Bensonhurst, Brooklyn, his father took me to task for calling them Italians in an essay I wrote a few years ago. "We are not Italians," he said. "We are Americans."

"Not even Italian Americans?" I asked, as I pierced the shrimp and squid and seafood and ate the cheese ravioli, a traditional ritual in this family that no meat is to be eaten until after Midnight Mass.

"No," he said with some anger and indignation in his voice. "We are Americans. My parents and grandparents came from Italy, and they became Americans. They never looked back. There is nothing Italian about us," he said loudly.

I raised my voice too, though I usually speak softly in his presence, deferring to his dominance as I think he wants me to. My son-in-law later told my daughter that I didn't show "respect" for his father in his own house, and that if I wanted to argue with his father, I should have done it in his, my son-in-law's house, and not in his father's house.

Were those expectations for my behavior not Italian American? Were not the foods we were eating and the rituals we were observing Italian American? My son-in-law refuses to watch *The Sopranos*, about an Italian American mafia family in New Jersey. "I don't watch those kinds of shows," he says. He won't tell me why not, but I presume it has to do with negative stereotyping of Italian Americans as Mafioso. The exchange prompted me to begin to think about the Finnishness of my own Americanness.

Was my Christmas Eve outburst, my uppity behavior, part of the Finnishness of my Americanness? The matriarchal family, I have been told, is quite commonly a residue of our ancestors in our lived lives. How our parents and grandparents conducted their family discourses influences the conduct of each of our family discourse. I begin to think of the girls I grew up with who shared my Finnish heritage, and whose grandparents all emigrated in the early 1900s, just as all four of mine did.

Strong mothers, silent fathers. Our mothers took on the mantle of 1950s ideal womanhood, though, and most of them did not do the strong stuff our grandmothers did -- keep boardinghouses for young men from Finland who came to seek their fortune in the mines; keep a few cows; have a milk business; work in a co-op store; cook, clean, and scrub while ruling their sons and daughters with shame and guilt as weapons. As my mind casts back over all the Finnish American families I knew, the gender of parental dominance was not something that could be generalized, for among my girlfriends and boy friends, the families seemed to have differently dominant parents.

There was the scared, silent Finnish American mother who wouldn't let her son play on the bluff, who always called for him if he strayed more than a hundred yards from her view; we called him, sadly, a sissy. There was the loud, boisterous Finnish-American miner father who always knew the latest joke, who could sing bawdy songs in three languages, English, Finnish, and French-Canadian, and who encouraged us kids to swear in Finnish. "*Saatana*!" We followed him as if he were a pied piper.

There was the social-climbing Finnish American mother whose daughters always had the latest fashion, and who didn't like them to keep company with kids who were probably not going to go to college.

There were my own parents, my shy artist mother and my shy welder father who bought me all the latest softball equipment, who brought me "steelies" from the shop so I could play (and lose all my) marbles with the boys. There was the in-the-house family behavior where he would say, "Where's the sugar, Pearl?" when it was closer to him than to her, and she would get up from her place at the table, go to the counter, and take him the sugar to go with his daily 4 o'clock after-work coffee.

Is the Finnishness in my Americanness in my nostalgia for saunas, fruit and pea soup, home-made coffee bread? My mother, in her 80s, bakes and sends us cardamom bread, rye bread, and potato bread, for our birthdays and holidays. Yet she also bakes pasties and saffron bread, and we hunger for those as much as for the more traditional Scandinavian fare. Our Cousin Jack (nickname for Cornish) childhood companions probably throw a little cardamom into their coffee bread, also. And the sauna? Doesn't everyone have a sauna nowadays? What matters the ritual that develops? It's part of a family's ethos to develop its own rituals and to change the rituals that they have been given, to make them their own. No — neither food nor baths makes me Finnish-American rather than American-Finnish.

In teaching about the Piaget stages of childhood development, I often tell my undergraduates a story based on my Finnish Americanness. I tell them we are going to study the terms *schema*, *assimilation*, and *equilibration*, and say, "In my family we take a bath together. Now, ask me questions."

The students ask, "Is it a jacuzzi?"

"No," I say.

"Is it a shower?"

"No," I say. They recoil in shuddering disgust. How could an up-standing middle-aged professor like me take a bath with her daughter, and even with her son when he was a young boy? By the time we are finished with the lesson they have absorbed into their schema of "bath," through the processes of "assimilation" and the reaching of "equilibration," the term and custom of "sauna," as practiced by my family. Is this how I am Finnish-American?

My daughter, when she attended college where I teach, said her friends, after that lesson, came up to her and said, "Do you really take a bath with your mother?" And she smiled and said, "Yes, I do. What's wrong with that? We wash each other's backs and tell stories."

Is it in the mixing of northern Michigan, Upper Peninsula, roots with Finnish background? We grew up, many of us, with our Finnish names and our aunts who belonged to the Kaleva Club, and our grandparents who put out the good tablecloth for the Finnish Church's *pappi* who came to minister to them when they emigrated. We were in a large eth-nic group, not alone, and we heard tales and grew up in towns with pub-lic saunas. We were encouraged to marry and date Finnish boys because if you marry a Catholic they make you change your religion, girls. So, girls, even if those Italian boys like the Finnish girls "stick with your own kind/cling to your own kind" as they sang in *West Side Story*, or your children will be half-breeds. I was actually told this by my aunt when I fell in love with a boy who wasn't of Finnish background.

Is it in the Finnish songs we sang in the Suomi College choir, songs I can still sing but whose words I don't understand--*Oi muistatko vielä sen virren*. Is it in the sentiment for the land, its forests, iron hills, its blue lakes and deep snows, its difference and its wilderness? Or in the Finnish community dances my sister's friend attended but which we never did, disdaining them?

Is the Finnishness of my Americanness in my deep interest in Fin-nish mythology? It is a fact that people ski in my dreams. As a person who is fascinated with the Jungian idea of the collective unconscious, and as a student of mythology weaned on the Greeks, I don't dream of sunny temples of marble and deep blue "wine dark" seas. I sometimes have what I call "archetypal" dreams. One of my dreams a few years ago featured a shack in the woods with a light shining on the snow. As I skied up, the man leaning on the shack told me his name was "Pent-ti." I didn't know anyone named Pentti. A few weeks later, at an edu-cation conference, I met a Finnish professor named Pentti. I have kept him as a friend, and we lunch and discuss Finland when we meet at other conferences. He appeared in my skiing dream before he appeared in my life.

I would be surprised if a deep consciousness of snow, Finnish names, and skiing pervades the archetypal dreams of people whose ancestors lived on more sunny shores. Is the Finnishness of my Americanness my resonance with themes of the woods, of cool lakes, of northern vistas? Is it my deep satisfaction now, as I am writing this, looking out my window at the new-fallen snow of January, and my deep dissatisfaction with our warm, snow-less December?

I just got a letter from a woman who was given my book, *A Location in the Upper Peninsula*, by her daughter. She tells me about growing up in Ishpeming, and in the location I write about in the book. She writes from Sun City in California: "I haven't been in the U.P. at wintertime since 1941. Even Ohio was too cold for me. I love the sunshine, year around. . . . I always dreamed of living in a place like this while growing up in the U.P." She doesn't have dreams where shadowy, mythologically-oriented people ski, obviously. Yet she is as Finnish-American as I am.

Is the Finnishness about that heavy $85.00 book, *A Sibelius Companion*, I bought in the bookstore at the University of Georgia last week? Did I buy it because I want to understand why my heart-strings soar as the octaves sing in the 3rd movement of his 5th symphony? Why do I have to keep turning up the volume on my stereo when that movement comes on? Why does that music touch something deep in me? I put the Saraste Finnish Radio Symphony Orchestra version into the CD Rom of my computer as I write this. I listen. The strings are quivering; the brass is striding; the tympanies underscore, the tempo slows, my heart races.

I grab the computer speakers and put one to each ear, as I cannot turn the volume loud though. As a musician friend of mine says, "I want to crawl into the speakers to where the music is." Sibelius, when inspired to write the 5th, said, in his diary of 1914, "God opens His door for a moment and His orchestra plays the fifth symphony." (p. 233, Ekman biography).

Finland declared a national holiday for Sibelius' fiftieth birthday, in 1915, when his 5th symphony premiered. He continued to revise it, and another "final version" was performed in 1916, and then the Russian revolution spilled over into Helsinki, leading to massacres, bombardments, shootings of officers, the imprisonment of his brother, and self-imposed exile at Järvenpää. He worked on it more, revising and revising. We who listen see what is to come as World War I begins and ends. I sob at the prescience and the beauty and the incipient terror. Then the resolution and the question in the anticipation of those last four chords calm me and make me fear at the same time.

But then Aaron Copeland's *Appalachian Spring* does that to me, as does the violin of Ann-Sophie Mutter, the voice of Kiri Te Kanawa, the piccolo runs in "Stars and Stripes Forever," and the congregation singing "The Lord's Prayer" as we do for a month or two each spring, before Lent. My graduate students when I taught in Finland a few years ago gave me as a parting gift, a CD of cellos playing Led Zeppelin, and my head bobs and my feet tap, too, when I listen to this fine fierce music. Music is part of me and always has been, and I sing, play, and listen as part of my training and background of 8 years of piano and many years of choir work.

Perhaps I am Finnish-American because of my Lutheranism. I felt deep relief in the white church in Helsinki when the Suomi College choir sang for the Lutheran World Federation, in 1963, and I confessed my sins (of being pregnant without being married yet -- a situation in which my maternal great-grandmother found herself, only she never married, and my grandmother probably emigrated because of the shame. Oddly, I was born on December 19, the same day as this maternal great-grandmother, Anna Kärnä, of Vimpeli). I then took Holy Communion from the then-president of the American Lutheran Suomi Synod, from the hands of my friend's father, Dr. Raymond Wargelin. I felt forgiven, and do, every time I participate in the Lutheran liturgy.

After many years in my young adulthood not going to church, I came home to the liturgy after personal troubles. But I felt the same at Catholic Mass, in the Cathedral de Notre Dame in Paris a few years ago, with a Latin liturgy and a French priest. And I prefer the church I go to now, in Ohio, of German origins, to my own Bethel Lutheran Church in Ishpeming, of Finnish origins, because of the music and the social activism of my present church, one of the most socially active in the Evangelical Lutheran Church of America.

Perhaps I am Finnish because of my socialist leanings. From a distance of continents and years, I read of the romantic sacrifice of the thousands of workers uniting against the Duchy rulers. I take second-hand nationalistic pride in the fact that the poor and the elderly are taken care of in this highly-taxed nation that still managed to pay its war debt. I absorb eagerly the details and translations that tell of how they fought off Stalin's troops for an impossible three months in 1939, recalling those brown-and-white photographs of the war in that picture book in Finnish that adorned the lamp table in my childhood home. I remember my pride when I lived in New York City, in reading Caro's book about Robert Moses, that the Finnish immigrants to the U.S. built the first co-op apartments in Sunset Park in Brooklyn. The co-op apartment is now a New York City institution. I drove past those first apartments, knowing their history and letting it resonate with mine.

Perhaps my Finnishness is in my love of clear glass and clean design, in how I have a collection of Iittala glass and gave Alvar Aalto vases to my sisters and children for Christmas one year. Perhaps it lies in the icicle candlesticks that adorn my dining room table, and of which my friends always say, "Where did you get those, Jane? They are so beautiful." Perhaps it was in the Marimekko wall hangings I stretched and placed on my house walls in the 1970s, and in the curvy-lined brown and white long dress I wear in many photographs from those days, bought at the Marimekko shop in Ann Arbor, Michigan. Perhaps it is in the $6.00 Marimekko wall hanging my half-Finnish daughter found at the Salvation Army store, which now adorns the wall in her town-house.

Perhaps my Finnishness is in my intellect, in my greedy reading of several translations of the *Kalevala*, and my attempts to attach *Kalevala* Runo lines to my own poems not composed consciously as echoing the *Kalevala*, but perhaps unconsciously composed that way; of my sub-scribing to a journal called *Books from Finland*; of my sitting on panels of Finnish American women at two international conferences to discuss education and creative writing; of my fondness for Finnish colleagues who study and visit at universities here; and of my collaboration with them in my own scholarly work; or perhaps it is in my reading and study of Finnish history (translated into English). I refused, when I was given a chance as a freshman at the only Finnish-American heritage college on the continent, to formally study Finnish, and I have regretted it ever since.

I had coffee with a professor of journalism while I was in Finland. We went to a sweet shop and took our pick from the delectable pas-tries. When I commented on Finnish baking, he sadly shook his head and said, "English is such an impoverished language compared to Fin-nish. In Finnish I have just the word to describe what you are saying, but English doesn't contain such a word." Can a person even *be* Fin-nish without the language, is a question I wonder about. Since the Finns defined themselves by language, and became a nation by lan-guage, can we be Finnish with our mother tongue being not Finnish, but English?

What influence does language structure have on the developments of one's ways of thinking and being? The Finnish mother tongue is spoken by people in a nation of only five million people, on a land mass the size of Minnesota, and because of the accident of my grandparents' immigration during hard times in the early twentieth-century, my mother tongue is English, rapidly becoming the language of choice throughout the world of commerce and culture. Part of my becoming American was becoming a native speaker, acquiring the American id-iom, and not learning Finnish. My coffee partner was not a native speaker of English and I doubt that the English language is less rich than the Finnish language. His comment illustrates how important lan-guage is to development of consciousness and being.

Perhaps my Finnishness is in my creativity. A Finnish scholar told me that poets in Finland come from Kuopio, where my maternal grandfather was born and raised. But not every Finnish American with roots in Kuopio writes poetry, so that is not a logical argument. And most of my ancestors came from the west, Vaasa. Someone told me my name means something very creative, and when I look it up on the world wide web, I see a lot of references to overhead projectors and such. It means "a creative line, as in drawing," someone told me. But my mother is the visual artist, and her maiden name was Eskelinen. Her father was from Kuopio.

Perhaps my Finnishness is in my reputation as a Finnophile. Recently, when an article appeared in the *New York Times Magazine* about the pervasive presence of Finns in the classical music world, I received copies in the mail from two far-away friends who had read it. "Dear Jane: Thought you would enjoy this. Love, Sara," wrote my Jewish American girlfriend from New York. "Dear cousin," said my first-cousin from Boston, who sent me a xeroxed copy. "I thought of you when I read this." I regularly receive such clippings from friends who know me and my Finnish interests.

Perhaps the Finnishness of my Americanness is only in my body. "The map of Finland is written across your face," someone told me when I worked in New York City in a mostly Jewish-populated school for bright children. I see a photograph of my stout paternal grandmother with her hands on her hips in exactly the angle in which they reside on my hips in a picture of me taken in front of Egyptian pyramids. My own stoutness seems unbeatable by diet, exercise, or will. I remember her gulping quarts of strawberry pop and think of that when I lug in twelve-packs of diet raspberry soda. The family female diabetes seems to have skipped me so far, but has come to rest in my younger sister's body. The family alcoholism in males of both sides is a warning to all of us.

Perhaps it is in my blood. I read that Finns are genetically similar to other Europeans and to central Russians. I look at my own descendant, my granddaughter. The light eyes of my daughter's family have been genetically overcome by the dark brown eyes of her father's family. Her blood is, one-half Italian European blood, one-fourth Finnish European blood, one-sixteenth French, one-sixteenth German, and one-eighth Austro-Prussian. Her small nose, her brown hair are her mother's. Her long lanky trunk her father's. She is a European American. Not a Finnish American, not an Italian American. Her Finnish genes have mixed with her other European genes, and she is an American. The old ties I feel to the land of my grandparents' birth were loosened in my children and may be all but severed in my grandchildren.

How many generations does it take to loosen these ties? In 1997, my sisters, cousin, mother and I were invited to a Finnish outdoor opera in Vimpeli, about a folk hero of Finland, Jakob (Jaakko) Ilkka, who with his men, fought off Swedish soldiers seeking to billet themselves in the area. Then we visited our Piirto family home, and on the grounds we found a monument with the saying, *Nvijamiehille 1597* ("For the Clubbers"). It turns out that the battle took place next to where our family lived, and we are supposedly related to this hero, according to an aunt we met, our father's first cousin, who looked just like our Aunt Lynn. We felt the forlorn yet proud tug of blood from four centuries ago, and, if a generation is twenty years long – 20 generations removed. What do the genetic researchers say about blood from 20 generations influencing descendants from rebel leadership during times of Swedish dominance that lived through the ages and were substantial enough to compel a modern opera?

As I chronicle all these ways I show my Finnishness in my Americanness, I realize that perhaps they all, together, make up the answer to my question. They all make up concrete details that contribute to a concept of soul. How am I a Finnish American? Let me count the ways. And when I go back next Christmas Eve, to my Italian-American family's feast of seafood, I will show my son-in-law's father this essay, and perhaps we can talk, peacefully, with mutual respect, American to American.

Marlene Ekola Gerberick

LETTER TO MY GRANDPARENTS

I don't think I've ever understood;
no, it's stronger than that.
I don't think I've ever *forgiven* you
for coming here.

For leaving places
with names like Evijärvi
and Töysä,
places where umlauts bounce
with the playfulness
of the midnight sun.

For going away forever
from birch defined land
on the shores of the Gulf of Bothnia
and then never, ever
stopping the longing for that land
left behind
so that none of us could forget
and become simply what we were;
inhabitants of a new land.

And, as I think of it,
if I hold anger toward the four of you
it is little in comparison
to what I feel for your children,
my parents,

who named us Marlene Lucille
and Colleen Grace and Helen Elizabeth
instead of Marja Liisa, Sigrid Aino
or Taava Miina;

who kept our mother tongue
hidden away in a dark closet
brought out only for visiting elderly aunts;
who insisted that this tongue
was for the dead and dying,
and, as if to confirm,
took us to church
to be harangued in Finnish from the ceiling
high pulpit
by elongated, bony ministers who
never stopped
while I grew ever more restive
chewed the back of the pew like a beaver,
counted the floorboards,
counted the steps to the altar,
hoped with all my might
that the minister would choke.

Yet with all their new country ways
your children, my parents, always
spoke the word Finland
as if they had said God.

They told your stories, with embellishments.
In retelling, the stories
became rainbow legends,
the basis of a new myth system
where all the deities lived
on the other side of a wide ocean.

And I, a child of even wider and deeper
imagination lived there with my gods
instead of here.

So that all my life
I have longed for the home
I've never seen,
sung myself to sleep with melodies
I've never heard,
warded off evil with incantations
spoken in a mother tongue

which I cannot even understand.

Burt Rairamo

THE IMMIGRANT

She only smiles,
can't speak English much.

She over-smiles
to cover up.

"When I smile
accept me better,
overlook my faults."

Her smile begs,
"can't you see
my smile speaks."

I speak to her
as if she understands.

She knows enough
to serve coffee, and donuts.
Were we the same,
when we arrived?

A SAUNA JUNKET AT LAKE WILCOX

It was Thursday evening, July 1959, when the phone rang!

"You want to go to the sauna Friday?" asked my friend Kenny on the blower.

"Where do you want to go?" I asked.

"Why don't we go to Lake Wilcox again?"

"Who else should we ask?"

"Osku, Jerry, Pulteri and Blueberry, and then the car is full!"

"What time?"

"I'll pick you up around six o'clock."

"See you then!"

I had almost left my home when Kenny called. I had been on my way to meet Olli to go swimming at the YMCA on College Street, downtown Toronto. The call now caused my thoughts to reflect upon the coming sauna trip and on Kenny. Next week it would be four years since I met Kauko, whom we now call Kenny. I had just moved to Canada the day before. Kauko delivered a newspaper, the *Telegram*, to Elsie's downtown three-story redbrick Victorian-style house, which had become our first, temporary home in Canada. Kauko was becoming established in his new environment and already had himself a newspaper route in the Lower Rosedale neighborhood, which he bicycled once a day. It was such a happy coincidence to meet another Finnish teenager of the same age so soon. I was a month or two older than Kauko. We immediately had to determine who was older. In those days, age was of great importance. It was the way with us boys then. That is how Kauko became my first friend in Canada.

It was at Elsie's house I heard for the first time "Fingelska" being spoken. In her loud sandpaper voice, Elsie would refer to the "front room" as a *ronttiruuma* and the "backyard" as a *takajaarti*. Her Finnish, over the years, had become quite heavily sprinkled with "Fingelska" expressions. It was July, the hottest summer that Elsie could remember, so hot that you could boil eggs on the asphalt on Yonge Street, as the temperature hovered around 30°.

Lake Wilcox was a favorite destination with us boys seeing that there were two or three saunas on a lake run by Finns and it gave us a nice drive as well. Driving around was one of our favorite forms of entertainment. The car became almost as our clubhouse. Kauko had already gotten his own life started in Canada. He had landed himself a promising apprenticeship in the printing business and managed to save the down payment for a 1948 shiny black two-door Ford. It had impressive wide white-wall tires - white walls were quite a special feature then- and a good radio. Radio was an all-important feature. Often we would be standing around, leaning on his car with all its windows open, radio blasting, listening to popular music such as Fats Domino's *"I found my thrill --- on Blueberry Hill --- on Blueberry Hill --- where I found you..."*One surprising thing to the rest of us about Kauko was that he had already begun dating local Canadian girls, although plenty of eligible Finnish girls were hanging around him. He had that mysterious good-guy/bad-guy appeal, which in later years became associated with James Dean. This combination of Kenny and his car attracted a lot of girls. In those days, owning a car was quite a status symbol. "Let's go for a drive!" he would holler, waving at some of his eager teenage followers.

I wondered who would bring the refreshments for the sauna? Maybe Osku! Everybody liked quiet Osku. He was so good-hearted that he actually had given somebody a shirt right off his back. The red-haired, freckle-faced, slightly red-eyed Osku lived downtown with his aunt and uncle, who had sponsored him to Canada as almost adopted but in fact just living with them. We always wondered if he was a real orphan but never asked. It was an unwritten rule of honor among us not to ask any personal questions. That was not manly. We had no past unless we voluntarily divulged some of it. We lived in the present only, the future was too far in the distance. It was enough just to be a Finn, no other qualifications were needed or necessary. Osku had learned a trade already in Finland as a lathe operator and was making good money, about $40.00 a week, working for a metal fabrication shop owned by a Finn. As Osku was a bachelor and had a good job earning good money, he bought himself a sensational car, a white Pontiac convertible with a blue folding top. The car had Finnish colors. Most of the time, when Osku showed up, the car was immediately surrounded by flocks of admirers and its hood was propped open. Boys wanted always to check the engine and comment on its power. It was the masculine thing to do. Everything was well with Osku except one thing, his liking for stronger types of beverages. To this end he kept an extensive array of samples in the trunk of his car at all times. Then one day the inevitable happened, he ran into a telephone pole in the middle of the night, coming back from a dance from Udora summer camp where the annual spring dance was held in a great big barn type building. The pole fell on his car and missed Osku only by inches, the car was a total write off.

"It is good that we are going in Kenny's car", I thought!

I heard a car horn outside and saw from the window that Kenny had already arrived and was waiving at me to hurry up. It seemed we were always in a hurry. I grabbed my bathing suit and a towel and ran outside. I had planned, in my mind, to sit in the front but it was already full. The front seat held always more importance. I jumped into the back seat next to Jerry and before we realized, as everyone was chattering, we were climbing up Yonge Street north, towards Richmond Hill.

Jerry, as his name bespeaks, was becoming Canadianized in a hurry. We never did find out his original Finnish name, he was always just Jerry. He was the shortest and the slimmest of us all, with black curly hair and a dark complexion, quite a favourite with the ladies. We always wondered if he had some gypsy blood in him. He was the first one of us to have a steady Canadian girlfriend, a jet-black-haired, chocolate-eyed Italian-Canadian called Patsy. We eyed stealthily this foreign-looking, English-speaking, dark-haired beauty only from a distance. Although we wanted to but we didn't dare to speak to her for fear we would have to respond in our broken English. We would lose face and be ashamed of our linguistic inadequacy for days to come. It was far better to avoid these situations by saying nothing. These English-speaking girls that we called "*kieliset*" seemed so different and mysterious to most of us naïve and simple country boys. But Jerry was different. He already spoke English and to our astonishment with practically no accent.

Pulteri also sat in the back seat. He preferred the back of the car where he could hide a bottle of beer and keep an eye out for the police at the same time. As soon as we past Finch Avenue, just outside the heavily populated Toronto, in spite of the roar of complaints from the rest of us in the car, Pulteri opened a bottle of O'Keefe, tucked it between his legs and nursed it slowly all the way. It was this sense of defiance against the rules of society that heightened his individuality at least in his own eyes. Pulteri was the craziest one of us all. He had recently arrived from Finland and had the latest Finn jokes and yarns. His face was chubby with a pimplish, oily skin but always full of smiles. Without any prompting ever, he kept telling us the funniest jokes and witty stories. We laughed and always waited for more. One important things in organizing a sauna trip like this was to invite as many jokesters and funsters as possible. To get laughs was an important element. Blueberry was another funny guy with all kinds of stories and was always invited. The sauna was in itself just a destination, a reason to get together, and once that was established, then it was important to have laughs.

Pulteri's first passion was cross-country motorcycle racing. It was his life. He amazed us with his endless tales and chronicles of the many hair-raising near-accidents and actual crashes he had been involved in. We often talked about him with strange awe and adulation, "he is such a daredevil he would, if dared, drive at full speed straight into a brick wall." He always dressed the same way, in a black leather jacket adorned with shiny silver stars and buttons, black jeans with a huge belt buckle with a motorcycle engraved on it, and black boots with metal toes and cleats. Pulteri had a part-time job pumping gas at an Esso station owned by a Finn on Lakeshore Road near the Canadian National Exhibition. Often on Sundays, with the Lord's Day Act in full effect, when everything except churches were closed, we would drop over to see Pulteri. We would lean against our car, listen to its radio and watch Pulteri at work and laugh at the stories he delivered in between serving customers. It never mattered whether the stories were true or not as long as they were funny. Making us laugh was his life's second ambition and we enjoyed being made to laugh. Some of us were not storytellers but only good laughers. Under an old, beat-up, wooden desk at the gas station, the kind we see in all gas stations, Pulteri always kept a case of O'Keefe well hidden and unbeknownst to the owner, for emergencies, as he explained it. With Pulteri as with Jerry we never asked for his real name, as nothing else could suit him as well as Pulteri.

We were now closing in on Lake Wilcox, nearing the famous Yonge street curve, about five miles from the lake. Through the entire trip, Blueberry occupied the prestigious front seat and kept turning the radio tuner back and forth endlessly. His job was to find us good music on the car radio. He was our music expert, as most of us others were not yet all that familiar with Canadian pop music. After all, Blueberry was a musician himself; he played drums, the accordion and a mellow alto saxophone. He often played at Saturday night dances, gigs as he called them, at Finn, Estonian and Polish halls, such as the Huron Hall, Udora Summer Camp, Eesti Maja, Don Hall and Polish Hall, with his brother Merv who picked the guitar and sang and his dad who played a button accordion. In those days, we never thought about these halls as being "white", "red" or "pink" halls, we simply went where the girls were. Politics were not part of our life and we left them to the older generation. Blueberry had gotten his nickname from the fact that he was born near Sudbury, where Ontario's best blueberries grow. The name stuck. Blueberry, being a third-generation Finnish Canadian with flawless English, acted as our spokesman and translator, and we gladly let him look after all discussions, negotiations, and purchases where and when English was required. We were always amazed at how well he spoke Finnish, even though he had never even seen Finland.

All of a sudden, Blueberry found an Elvis Presley song. "Everybody quiet, listen to this", he said, and we listened *"Don't be cruel to a heart that's true. --- Why should we be apart? --- I really love you baby --- Cross my heart"*. Then came the Everly Brothers singing: *"Bye Bye love - -- Bye Bye happiness --- Hello loneliness --- I think I am gonna cry."* We sang along as best we could and pretended that we knew the words, but in reality, we mostly just hummed along. However, afterwards it always made us feel a little more Canadian.

Now we turned off Yonge Street to the South Lake Road, which circled the Lake Wilcox, and in minutes, we saw a large wooden sign "SAUNA" high on a steel post. We noticed the lake below the road on the left and a large rectangular, well-trimmed grass-carpeted property sloping gently towards the lake. We saw a large white frame main building down below on the right and two or three small white independent sauna cabins by the shore, from which a long narrow deck stretched far into the small lake. The lake itself was only about half a mile wide and one mile long but it was the closest clean lake to Toronto.

Many Finnish newcomers to Toronto would escape the city and its blistering heat to come here on weekends to spend a day picnicking, sunning, gossiping, swimming and taking a sauna. These new immigrants hadn't yet been able to save enough money to buy themselves a cottage lot, and most didn't own a car yet, but always had a friend with wheels to bring them.

All cars were parked in neat parallel rows on both sides of the lawn, with their trunks facing one another. The babies, Coleman coolers and picnic baskets were offloaded from the car and placed on blankets laid down on the grass. Children played, women gossiped and men wandered around exchanging news from the old country and swapping their work experiences in Toronto. The sauna owners charged $1.00 per day for parking and another dollar for a sauna. They also sold soft drinks, coffee and *pulla*.

There were other saunas on the lake as well, but you always went to the Haanpää sauna, the one you knew of and recommended. The other side of the lake, the north side, was flat. The ground was only a few inches higher than the lake and it was often flooded in the spring. It was said that if one ran out of stronger beverages, a bootlegger or as we called it *"koiratorppa"*, could be found on that side of the lake.

Blueberry was the only one of us who didn't like taking a sauna or swimming. He would never waver to our constant prompting and adamantly kept his clothes on tight at all times but instead supervised our dressing room and our beverages while the rest of us took several saunas and swam. From the dressing room, he shouted out jokes and funny stories and, in this way, he didn't miss any laughs himself from the other jokesters.

We roared all night in a continuous uninterrupted laughter from the never-ending jokes and stories. Some of us swam and most of us took several saunas. The cottage and its immediacy filled with happy raucous voices pushing the darkness of the night a little further into the beyond and drowning out the evening calls of the crickets which were trying to compete with us for attention.

As the bright moon appeared high above Lake Wilcox and lowered its silvery moonbeams across this small lake, thus ended the sauna outing for a group of immigrant teenage boys in the late 1950's. We were eagerly experiencing life in Canada but much of it still within a Finnish context although the inevitable changes were seen and felt coming to all of us, to some faster than to others.

Helen Koski

SUDBURY

What, this is my home,
A cold, rough chunk of wax,
This beehive in a zone
Of barren hill, whose
Belly swarms with
Moonless tunnels?

What, should the roof
Collapse o'er all, could man
Show this deep void as proof
Of stolen rock, whose
Heart hardens with
Molten fever?

Ah, formless whole,
A withered stem and leaf
Embrace my inert soul
With gentle arms, whose
Touch moulds home with
Yielding stone.

KIRSTI

Evening, sitting quietly
In hidden niche,
Tunes
Taut fiber, feels
Notes with textured pitch.

Lamplight, bending busily
O'er eager loom
Grasps
Spun baton, threads
Songs with patterned tune.

Yellow, vibrant melody
Of petalled bronze,
Beats
Muted red, counts
Staffs of criss-cross yarn.

PART THREE:

Connecting with Memory and the Self

Lynn Maria Laitala

TAMARACK AUTUMN

It was a lovely, warm Indian summer day. I sat on my porch, waiting and rocking. Emily was coming. The grandchild, the golden child.

My yard was tidy, ready for winter snow. I had dug up the dahlias and mulched the tulips. The roses were covered too. I'd raked the fallen leaves from the grass.

Beyond the yard the fields were no longer tidy. Fields that Arvo and I had cleared and tended were being reclaimed by the woods. Tamarack and alder had moved in; now the tamarack was flaming gold. It brought its own light to the low places.

A car turned into the driveway, and then Emily was bounding up the porch steps. I started to rise but Emily threw her arms around me as I sat in my rocking chair.

"Oh Mummu, how good to be home!"

Emily's serious young man was standing uncomfortably behind her. He reminded me of the young Lenin. He must have worked hard at the likeness, with his high collar and the little wire-rimmed glasses. He extended his hand formally.

"How are you, Peter?" I asked.

"Pekka," he said.

"Yes, Mummu. Peter is studying Finnish at the university. He changed his name to Pekka."

"My major field is American history, of course. My specialties are immigration and labor," Peter-Pekka told me.

"Mummu, Pekka wants to interview you on the tape recorder. About Grandpa and the 1916 strike. He's writing his dissertation about the strike."

The old terror stirred in me. I'd thought that when Urho died I buried the tragedy with him, but here was this humorless young man looking for his history, bringing back the dread of 53 years as fresh as if a policeman were here on my porch, come to take me away.

Emily sat with her head leaning against my knee, just as she had as a child. I stroked her hair. Peter-Pekka had already turned on his recording machine.

"Aina Lahti; subject Mesaba Strike of 1916: date of interview, September 19, 1969: Pekka Johnson, Interviewer," he said tonelessly into the microphone. He began to ask questions in a strange, stilted Finnish that I couldn't understand.

"I'm sorry," I said. "I know my English isn't good, but too many Finnish words have changed. My Finnish is so different from yours."

Peter-Pekka looked disappointed but he switched to English without comment. I couldn't think of how to stop him. I could only tell him what he wanted to hear. He asked where I was born in Finland and how I came to this country. I explained that I came with my older brother Arvo.

"Why?"

"It seems silly now. We wanted adventure. We were young. American streets were supposed to be paved with gold."

"Do you remember Ellis Island?"

"What I remember better is crossing the North Sea to Liverpool. I didn't believe anyone could be so sick and live. And then Ellis Island, yes, and then the train trip to the Mesaba. Others from our village had gone before. They found us a place in a boardinghouse. I worked there in the kitchen as a maid. Arvo went to work in the mine. The streets were dirty with the red dust of the iron ore, not paved with gold.

"How did you meet your husband, Urho Lahti, hero and martyr of the Strike of 1916?"

For a moment I permitted myself to remember Urho as he was when I first saw him. He lived in the boardinghouse. He was very handsome, but there was something else about him - a kind of fire from within. I mistook his fervor for love. How easily I married him. After we were married I learned that his passion was of himself and that it quickly found new objects. Not women. Ideas. I didn't tell this to Peter-Pekka. Only how we met in the boardinghouse.

Peter-Pekka wanted to know about the conditions that gave rise to the strike. Yes, the work was dirty. Yes, the conditions were bad. Yes, pay was low. Peter-Pekka warmed to his sense of injustice and the glory of the protest. Urho would have liked this boy. They could have fed each other's anger, talked injustice for hours on end. They might have been striking comrades.

"Can you tell me anything about the way Urho died?"

There it was. Slowly I shook my head.

"He was killed by company goons and left in a ditch by the side of the road, isn't that true?" Peter-Pekka demanded.

"Yes, he was found dead by the road. It wasn't determined who had killed him."

"Wasn't it reasonable to assume that it was the company goons, considering his leadership position in the strike?"

"That's what was assumed."

Peter-Pekka was disappointed because I gave him no more, but he had had me say on his tape machine what he wanted to hear. After a few more questions, he shut it off and stood to stretch his legs. He looked about him, seeing the old farm for the first time. His eyes settled on the tamaracks below.

"What's blighting those fir trees?" he asked Emily.

She smiled at him. "Those are tamaracks. They look like evergreens with their needles, but they aren't. They loose their needles every year, after the other trees have lost their leaves. But for a while right now they really light up the woods. It's one of my favorite trees."

"I'm going to have a look." With a glance Peter-Pekka commanded Emily to accompany him. She started to rise, but I put my hand on Emily's shoulder.

"Sit here a little while with your old Mummu," I said. I smiled at Peter-Pekka apologetically. He turned and strode down the porch steps.

"He's very brilliant, Mummu," Emily said when he had gone. "I'm glad that he's going to include Grandpa in his history."

"Emily ..." I began. "Emily ..." I tried again.

"Mummu?"

"The history in books . . . . It isn't the history in life."

"I know, Mummu. I study history, too, you know. I know how limited we are by the sources, and . . ."

"Emily ... I'll tell you what happened to your grandfather."

Emily became very still.

"They say that the Finnish women knew that their men were doomed when they went off to fight the Russians. The women knew, but the men still went."

"But Finland maintains its independence today because all those men were willing to die."

"Yes. And that's how it was with the strike as well."

"You mean you knew it was doomed? Weren't you a socialist, too?"

"I knew we couldn't win the strike."

77

"But if people hadn't been willing to strike over and over again for an eight-hour day and better conditions, they never would have gotten reform."

"Yes, that's true. That's what Urho wanted to die for."

"Isn't that what he died for? Mummu?"

"It's easier to find two sides in history than in life."

"Mummu?"

It was hard to begin to speak of things that I had never spoken of, but I didn't have much time. Peter-Pekka was upon the tamaracks and beginning his inspection.

"Andy, your father, was only three. The strike had gone on for months.

There was little fuel. We were nearly out of food on very short rations.

There was no milk for the baby. We were losing the strike. Urho only knew how to fight, he didn't know how to lose. He became obsessed. He worked day and night, went to endless meetings, tried to keep spirits up against certain defeat. But at home - when he came home - he grew angrier and angrier."

That awful night lived fresh in my memory. I could almost smell the smoky kerosene lamp that burned dimly near the window when Urho burst in the door.

"The night he died," I continued, "he was very angry. He was feeling the despair he never showed outside our house. The baby was crying. He was always hungry and he often cried. Urho came in, walked right over and slapped him. I ran to push Urho away from the baby. Urho turned on me and began to hit me. All the anger over the strike. He hit me and hit me. And then Arvo burst in..."

"Uncle Arvo?"

"Yes, of course. Arvo came in and tried to pull Urho off me. They fought. In the fight Urho's head hit the edge of the cookstove. I didn't see how it happened. But Urho lay still and there was blood on the stove."

"He was dead?"

"Yes."

"Daddy saw Uncle Arvo kill his father?"

"Yes."

"What did you do then?"

"Arvo took his body out in the middle of the night and put him in the ditch. Of course everyone thought that the company had him killed."

"Don't cry, Mummu," Emily said quietly. She put her arms around me.

Peter-Pekka was returning from his inspection, nearing the porch. He didn't notice my tears.

"Kind of a shabby tree, really," he said. "Mrs. Lahti, it occurred to me to ask you a few questions about life after the strike."

He flicked on his machine again.

"When did you move away from the Mesaba and up to Winton with your brother?" he asked. I was ready to answer.

"Just after Urho died. Arvo wasn't really with the strike, you know, but they blacklisted all Finns just alike. There was no work. Arvo liked farming better than mining anyway."

"Did they try to deport you as Mongols under the Oriental Exclusion Act?"

"Oh no. Not us. We got our papers without trouble. Maybe others had trouble."

"They tried to classify Finns as Mongols, who were seen as dirty yellow dogs." Peter-Pekka burned with anger at the history of oppression.

"How did you manage then, after the strike?" he persisted.

"Well, in Finnish they say, `When a cat has to climb a tree, it finds its claws.' We just lived. Milked cows. Planted potatoes. Arvo worked in the lumber camps in the winter. We got active in the Co-op."

Peter-Pekka lost interest in my story, and flicked off the recording machine. I was thinking of spring mornings scented of lilac and the long shadows of the midsummer evenings. I'd like to see another spring.

I thought. Peter-Pekka looked from his watch to Emily. Emily got up slowly.

"I'll come again soon, Mummu." She leaned down to lay her cheek against mine, and I felt its wetness.

"I won't tell, Mummu," she whispered.

"Don't cry, Emily," I told her, and then they were gone, and I sat alone in the fading afternoon, alight with the golden glow of the tamaracks.

CHILD OF THE PLACE

My parents came from Finland, first in a crowded boat over rough seas, then by railroad, tagged like pieces of baggage. My father went into the mine and my mother struggled with her grief, alone among strangers. The land of opportunity was bitter disappointment, but their children would do better, they said. It was all for the sake of the children.

My six brothers and sisters made my parents proud when they went to college. Some have two and three degrees. I'm the black sheep. My parents are ashamed because I followed my father into the mine.

My parents ask, why don't you leave Winton and go someplace where you could make something of yourself? I can't answer them. Maybe when I was a child I lingered too long in the soft light of a summer evening, popping wild cucumbers by the garden shed.

Maybe it was the smoky smell of birch heating the sauna stove on a crisp September day, or plunging into the lake when it was the bluest of blue, trimmed with autumn gold. Should I have left when the white-fish were running? Or when my blood rose with the tang in the November air at hunting time?

I didn't understand how anyone could leave, once they'd snow-shoed across Basswood Lake when it glittered in twenty below. And how could I leave the old people, speaking musical Finnish in the Co-op, in the post office? My parents say the immigrants were fools who expected to find streets paved with gold. They got hardship and misery. But if you go out walking in the early spring, when the marsh marigolds run riot, you will find the woods carpeted with gold.

My dad is crippled with arthritis so my boy Mike and I make firewood for the folks. One May afternoon I was over at their place stacking it, and stayed to have coffee and *pulla* with Mother after-wards. We sat on the porch, looking out over the empty fields on the edge of the village. Bright green leaves of birch and poplar budded out in the woods beyond. "Your brother Esa bought a new house, Frank," Mother told me in high, scolding Finnish. "He got promoted at his job. It's too late for you to make something of yourself, but Mike is taking after you. You should make him see there's no future up here."

"Let Mike live his own life, Mother," I said. "You got lots of other grandkids who can make you proud." Most of them couldn't be bothered to send her a Christmas card.

"Mike's smart. He takes after his mother. That girl would have been something if you hadn't ruined her life - getting her in the family way, making her drop out of college."

"I know, Mother," I said. "Helena could have been something."

I remembered the dark autumn day she'd come to my door, pregnant. Only Helena and I knew that Mike wasn't my baby, and I would have forgotten long ago if I wasn't reminded, like Mother reminded me now.

"Somebody told me that Mike's making moonshine. He's hanging out with the wrong crowd," Mother said.

I smiled. I'd made moonshine with Jake LaPrairie, Dave Rautio and Andy Lahti. It was serious business back then. Good to see the kids keeping up tradition.

"He'll be fine, Mother," I said. "I gotta go."

I walked home over Finn Hall Hill, past the empty lot where the Hall had been. I turned at the top to look back at the village below. It had changed over the years, but in some ways it hadn't changed at all. To the west, the tracks came out of the woods following the bend of the river. A kid was fishing from an old wooden skiff near Laitinen's public sauna. The sauna was closed now; Cecelia lived alone upstairs in the big blue metal-clad building.

Clapboards on the old false-fronted boardinghouses that lined the street were fading to rusty red and weathered gray. The few old bachelors they still housed had weathered, too. Jussi was sitting on a bench in front of Rautio's boardinghouse, leaning forward, cap tilted against the sun, elbows resting on his knees. A bunch of kids and a couple of dogs played in the street. Heikki was going home from the saloon, not too steadily. Old Mrs. Tanttari was on her way to the post office with a package.

To the east I could see where the river flowed into Fall Lake. In my mind I traveled north with the current, over Pipestone, through Newton, on to Basswood.

I felt good when I looked at Winton from the top of the hill. I sat there for a few minutes before I walked home in the spring evening, fresh with the scent of balm o'gilly.

Mike was in the backyard with Johnny Lahti, taking apart a 36 Chevy coupe. They were fine looking boys in their engineer boots, jeans and white t-shirts. Both wore their hair combed back with a curl falling over their foreheads. I marveled that their hair stayed in place even when they were working under the hood of the car.

"Hey Dad, give us a hand with this block," Mike called. I went over and wrestled with the tri-pod a while before Helena called us in to eat.

"I got a job driving truck on Four Mile for the summer," Mike said at supper.

"And then you can go to junior college in the fall," his mother said.

"Don't nag, Mom. I'm not going to college," Mike said. "Dad's gonna get me a job in the mine."

Helena glared at me. The girls looked scared, expecting a fight. Helena walked around the table, throwing scoops of mashed potatoes down, plate by plate.

"When does the job start, Mike?" I asked.

"Day after graduation."

"We won't have time to go on a fishing trip then."

"I'll skip a couple of days of school. Grades are in already, anyhow."

Helena slapped down slices of meat loaf. Then she stood back, hands on hips.

"What's the matter with you, Mike?" she said. "Do you really want to end up like him?" She jerked her head in my direction.

"Yeah, Mom. That would be fine," Mike said evenly.

Her face got ugly and contorted. She stared at Mike for a moment and then stormed out of the room.

"I'm going to college," Cindy whispered to Penny.

We finished supper in silence. Helena came back downstairs to make my lunch. I was on the graveyard shift, eleven to seven. We changed shifts every week. Even though I'd been at the Pioneer Mine for sixteen years, I never got used to switching shifts. I was always tired when I worked graveyard.

Helena was still tight with anger. I would have tried to comfort her, but I was what was making her hurt.

She packed meatloaf sandwiches in the lunch box with an apple and some date bars. Cindy and Penny cleared the table and washed dishes, trying to be invisible and good at the same time.

Helena turned to me, anger gone. She sounded tired.

"I'm sorry, Frank," she said. "You've been good to me. I just wanted more for Mike."

I shook my head. There was nothing I could say. The painful thing was that I loved Helena like I always had, helpless to defend myself. If there was more that Mike could have from this life than I had, it would be loving a woman who loved him back.

I went up to get a few hours rest before my shift.

I was proud to be a miner. I went down the mine at the beginning of World War Two as a general underground worker. Next I was a timber trammer. It took six years to work up to contract miner.

The Allies couldn't have won World War II without the ore from the Iron Range, and the U.S. wouldn't be the greatest country in the world if we hadn't won the war.

I was too upset to sleep, but I lay there until it was time to go to work. Then I walked around to the Old Winton Road and waited for my ride. It was a soft, clear spring night, with pockets of chill in the low places.

Bernie waited for me outside the mine-head. We'd been partners since 1948. You never called your partner by name, just Partner. I saw more of him than I did of Helena and we got along better, too, but then, we were clear about our job and how to get it done. Our lives depended on it.

The whistle blew at eleven sharp. We got in the cage and dropped 1300 feet in a minute and a half. I popped my ears without thinking about it.

The way it worked, there were six guys on a contract - two guys on each shift. The company gave you the contract and set the rate. If it was easy going you got paid less, hard work you got more, so it evened out.

We got paid by the ton, and the six men on the contract divided the pay for the contract equally. That meant we couldn't afford to tolerate anybody slacking off. We met our partners coming off swing shift in the tunnel.

"What's in the place?" I asked.

"It's ready to drill: you have to get the bits," one of our partners said. You could see he was proud of the fact they'd done a hard day's work.

We had good partners. One time Bernie and I were in a contract with a couple of guys who put a sloppy set. You can't be off a six-teenth of an inch when you set timber, or you're going to get some-body killed. Bernie didn't hesitate to let them know.

"Ever do that again and you'll wind up with an axe in your head," he told them. They shaped up.

We did cave mining in Pioneer, taking out ore six feet at a time. Set timber, drill, blast a cut and six feet would cave down. Hang a block on the last set of timber and work the scraper, scraping up all the loose ore out of the drift, and start again.

The conditions were always different. Maybe it was wet, and you had to wear rubber suits, which was miserable. Maybe when you blasted a piece of ore would fly down the drift like a cannon shot and hit one of the sprags – braces - on a set five back from the end of the tunnel, making five sets of timber come down. A mess. If it was real good going you could make a round in a shift, but in hard ground it might take more than one shift just to drill the holes.

We were drilling hard ground that night. Drilling is like being in an eight-foot square room with two fifty-caliber machine guns running steady for eight hours. When we had to communicate, my partner and I signaled each other with our headlamps. After the shift I couldn't hear myself speak when we met our partners coming on shift in the tunnel and told them what was in the place.

All of us contract miners get hard of hearing after a while. I felt real bad when I realized that I couldn't hear spring peepers trill or birds sing. I never could sleep in the daytime. The thing to do on a fine spring morning was to go fishing.

Helena gave me a meek smile when I came in the back door. She was making breakfast for me, like always. She did her job in the marriage. I did my job. That's how most marriages worked. Why did I feel so bad about it?

"Want to go fishing?" I asked.

She looked out the window at the fresh green world, and glanced back around the kitchen.

"Sure," she said. "I'll pack a lunch."

One of the things I loved about Helena was that she was always willing to go to the lake. We drove up the Fernberg Road to our cabin. A week before we'd done spring clean up and put the boat in the lake - a seventeen-foot Grumman with a three-horse Johnson motor. I carried the gas can down to the dock, Helena brought poles and bait and we bailed out the boat with a coffee can and a sponge.

We motored along the shore, Helena looking for signs of life at neighboring cabins. I looked out for deadheads. Back in the logging days, when inboard launches towed booms of logs across Fall Lake to the lumber mills in Winton, some of the logs sank. Now, fifty years later, they popped back up, darkly waiting to break the shear pin on my motor.

Several boats of fishermen bobbed at the edge of the churning waters at the bottom of the dam. Names of resorts were stenciled on most of the bows. It was a good spot to fish, especially if you hadn't gotten out to a quiet bay at dawn.

I cut the motor and Helena baited a hook for me. She liked to fish. It was something we still enjoyed together. Helena had her own reasons for wanting Mike to go on to college. She wasn't like my folks who wanted their children to achieve to make them look good. I hadn't realized how bad it hurt her to drop out of school when she got pregnant. She thought Mike would suffer the loss she had if he didn't go. She'd never been so angry about anything before.

Mike was a good student so she assumed he'd go on to college. The duck's ass haircut should have tipped her off. I could tell when Mike and his classmates decided whether they were going to leave or stay in the north way back in grade school. It didn't have anything to do with being smart, or getting good grades. It was something else. They started to dress differently from each other, talk different, make different kinds of jokes. Same when I was a boy.

Helena had loved school and I had loved the joy in her. I would never have taken it away.

While she fished, watching clouds pile up in magnificent thunderheads, I glimpsed the Helena I loved. I didn't want to break the mood, but later, after we'd caught our limit and were sitting on the bench by our dock eating lunch, I tried to talk to her.

"It's okay if Mike turns out like me," I said, " because I like my life. What you don't want, is for him to turn out full of regret, like you."

I'd worked to figure that out and it cost me to say it, but it came out wrong. Helena stuffed the lunch mess in the bag and stomped up the hill to the cabin. I finished my sandwich, watching gulls bob out in the lake.

Mike and I got in a quick trip to Basswood. We took the Grumman over Four Mile into Back Bay. Walleyes were biting. Mike's a good partner - quiet, patient, good sense of humor. He's got a real generous nature. When he was a little kid, he started fishing by himself off the White Bridge in Winton. He'd fish from the bridge all day if we let him. When Helena told him we couldn't eat so much fish, he brought fish to his grandma and her boarders and to the other widows in town. He knocked at their doors with one hand, holding his other arm straight up to keep the stringer up off the ground.

We sat on a ledge, listening to loons, having a smoke. I was thinking about Helena when she was young.

"You know any poems?" I asked Mike.

"Has Miss Gjervik let anyone get through Ely High School without memorizing poetry?" he asked. I laughed. I'd had her, too.

I recited some Chaucer.

Mike countered with "Sumer Is Icumen In," while the sun sank through mountains of clouds, changing from brilliant red to deep purple. If the sunset made music, it would have sounded like a pipe organ.

"Maybe those English poets got it right about their place," Mike said, "but this sure isn't England. Robert Service knew the north."

We recited Robert Service poems.

"I liked one Spenser poem," I told Mike. "How did it go? 'My love is like to ice, and I to fire...'"

"'How comes it then that this her cold so great/ Is not dissolved through my so hot desire/ But harder grows the more I her entreat?'"

Mike responded. "You must have been in unrequited love, too." He grinned a crooked grin.

Mike was in love with Kathy Chelik, but he was from the wrong family, went to the wrong church.

"So," he asked, "How long did it take you to get over it?"

They always say, oh, you're young, you'll get over it. Or, you're young, it's not serious. Bullshit.

"I didn't," I said.

"Oh," said Mike, light dawning. "You married her."

I thought I could prove my love, when Helena came to my door asking if I still wanted her. I thought my love would fix everything. I almost told Mike why I married his mother, that it wasn't my fault she ruined her life - and it wasn't his either, no matter what he did with himself. But as long as Mike thought he was my son, he was my son. I never wanted him to find out otherwise.

He was going to be sticking around, up on Four Mile this summer, down in the mine come fall. There'd be lots more fishing trips.

At the beginning of every summer, my brothers and sisters wrote to announce which week they planned to come up and stay at our cabin.

Helena, normally sociable, was getting annoyed. It was fun when the cousins played together in the lake, roasting hotdogs and marshmallows on the beach in the evening. But now the kids stayed home, and the adults came for solitude. They treated us like the maid and handyman at their own private resort.

Brother Esa - the one who had a big promotion and a new house - wrote that his wife wasn't coming this year, either. He was going to bring his boss up for some fishing.

"Third week in July. The nicest week of the summer," Helena said. "I bet he expects us to supply the food, too."

She was right. They arrived at the cabin in Esa's brand new Chrysler, equipped with nothing more than fishing tackle and beer.

"Frank, Helena. This is Bill Stevens." Esa introduced us to a man expensively dressed in woodsy clothes. Stevens extended his hand with a politician's smile.

"Pleased to make your acquaintance. Good of you to have me," he said.

"Come on up to the cabin," I said.

We sat in the wide screen porch I'd added to the original log structure, on comfortable wooden furniture Mike had built in shop. Esa passed out beer. I accepted. Helena declined. Stevens settled himself down with a satisfied sigh.

"God's country," he said, looking through the birch trees down to the lake. It was, as Helena had predicted, the height of summer glory.

"I used to come up here summers with my family when I was a boy," Stevens said. "Haven't been up for quite a while. Too long."

"Well, you've traveled all over. You can't be everywhere," Esa said.

"That's true. I found a nice little fishing lake way up in Canada. Have the whole lake to myself. Fly in at least once a summer. We like to go to Colorado in the winters. One thing about Minnesota, whole place is flat as a swamp. Earlier this year I was in the Andes. That was something else. Climbed peaks no one had ever climbed. You can't imagine," Stevens said, turning to me, "what it's like. Stepping where no man has stepped before."

"I can," I said. "It's not a big deal."

Esa glowered at me. Stevens turned red.

"I hardly imagine that you could have any idea what it's like," he said.

"If you ever did it, you'd know that there's no feeling like it in the world."

"I've done it," I said.

"You? When did you ever step where no man stepped before?" he challenged, looking around our modest cabin with contempt.

"Every day. After I blast out a chunk of rock 1300 feet underground and go in to set timber, I know I'm stepping where no man has stepped before."

"Frank!" Helena sounded like she was choking. Her face was twisted with distress. "I have to go home."

I rose and shook hands with Stevens, who radiated hostility.

"See you, Frank," Esa said curtly.

We drove in silence until just before the Garden Lake Bridge. Then Helena broke down in horrible sobs.

I'd never seen her cry before. I'd really done it this time.

"I'm sorry, Helena," I said.

She twisted around and lay her face on my leg. I put my hand on her hair.

"That was him," she said through the sobs.

"Who?"

"Stevens. He's Mike's father."

My hand froze where it was, there on her head. I concentrated on driving with the other hand. When we got to the boathouses I needed both hands to shift and make the turn to Winton.

I parked in the alley. Helena walked past the girls in the kitchen and straight upstairs.

"What happened to Mom?" Penny asked.

I sat down at the table. Cindy was sewing herself a dress, and Penny was making a doll from the scraps.

"The man Esa brought to the cabin hurt her feelings."

"Jeez," Cindy said.

"Yeah," I said. "I guess I'll go talk to her." I felt low as dog crap.

I went up and sat on the edge of the bed. Helena had rolled herself up in a blanket cocoon, still sobbing. I couldn't tell where my hurting left off and hers began. Her sobs tapered off.

"He didn't even recognize me," she whispered after a while. "I'm glad he didn't, but doesn't he remember? I know I've changed a lot, but Helena isn't that common a name. Wouldn't it jog his memory? God, he never thought about me or Mike at all. Just came up here, enjoyed himself. On to Canada, Colorado, the Andes. Yeah," she said bitterly, "he likes to go where no man has been before. Penetrate virgin territory." The sobs returned.

"I'll tell you what hurts worst, Frank," she said, struggling to get herself under control. "I thought I was in love with him. I wanted to marry him. How could I have been in love with that prick?" She pulled the covers off her face and looked at me with red puffy eyes.

"I never saw you cry before," I said. Or heard her use bad language. It scared me.

"I haven't cried since I found out I was pregnant with Mike," she said. She started sobbing again. "How could I have loved that terrible man?"

I lay down next to her and fumbled around in the blankets for her hand.

"That was the summer after our first year at junior college," I said. "I was working for the Forest Service. You were working at Maple Isle." I let myself go back in time.

"There never was a more beautiful summer," I said. "The long drought had broken, but it only rained at night. Every morning the world was fresh and clear. Every day was sunny, with just a gentle breeze. Basswood smelled of sun on pine and lichen. The cliffs were full of berries. The lake was warm, with miles of sandy beaches."

"We got together with kids from other resorts for bonfires on the beaches," Helena said.

I remembered Helena's easy, transparent joy.

"You loved the whole world, Helena. Bill was part of the world you were in love with. Mike was conceived from that golden Basswood summer."

Helena sat up. She looked at me in amazement.

"That's right, isn't it," she said slowly.

"*You've been too hard on yourself, Helena. You keep punishing yourself on account of one mistake.*"

"You never held it against me," she said.

"Why would I? Mike's a great kid."

"I don't want him to wreck his life like I did."

"Yeah. If you hadn't gotten pregnant you could have stayed single and taught English poetry to hoods with DA haircuts. Or maybe made a lot of money and gone mountain climbing in the Andes."

I thought I'd made her cry again, but no. She was laughing.

"God, is he a jerk," she said.

I rolled her over onto my chest, wrapped up in her blanket cocoon. She let me hold her there and rock her while her laughter changed back to sobs.

Eija I. Heward

THE PROVIDER

" **J** ust some tea, please," she whispered in a slight southern twang.

I scanned the one-room apartment, trying hard not to show my amazement. I had driven by this building hundreds of times and never imagined anyone could be living under such conditions in the middle of our comfortable, no posh, seaside community. I suddenly felt angry and wished to know who the landlord was, but I didn't ask. Instead, I decided to keep my coat on.

The furniture, if you can call it that, was scanty - a filthy gas stove with all the burners glowing. Obviously there was no heat. There was a grimy refrigerator, a bookcase lined with open cereal boxes, a few Ravioli cans and a half loaf of bread. There was a card table covered with sleazy magazines pushed against the frozen window panes that lined the entire wall. Two chairs seemed tossed in the direction of the table. Well-worn clothes drooped over both of them. An old TV sat in the dimmest corner at the far end of the room. Finally, there was the double-bed size mattress on the floor, where Barbara was lying, shaking violently.

I pulled the cord of the bare light bulb that hung from the peeling, water-stained ceiling. Seeing better, I now saw rock concert posters tacked on the wall behind Barbara's head. They were the only attempt at personalizing this place that I could see. A pungent smell of bacon and tobacco smoke had followed me from the restaurant below.

"Do you live alone?" I asked, as I brought over the tea and sat down on the mattress beside her.

"No, I have a boyfriend, Matt, who works at the Mobil Station on the corner. He's their mechanic. He loves me. We're pretty tight. He'd like to marry me, but..." her voice trailed off as she looked down, avoiding my eyes. She had been crying before I arrived.

I really looked at her now, this frail eighteen year old, this daughter of the most successful lawyer in town. No doubt she had attended the best private schools the Boston area could offer. This brown-haired, green-eyed beauty had stolen the heart of the police chief's son-in-law, or so it was rumored. This is what I knew of her when she replied to my ad. Small towns are full of rumors and I try hard to close my ears to them.

When she came for the interview, she presented herself as a competent, polished, well-controlled young woman. Even though she was young, she told me she no longer lived at home (which wasn't too unusual in a town like ours); and, she had had a few positions in church nurseries working with babies. She said she loved babies. That was easy to see too, as she talked. She had confidence, and she so wanted the job.

My wildly successful year old day care center needed another 'baby' person. I hired her after talking with only one of the policemen that happened by at the French pastry shop near my center. He seemed slightly taken aback when I asked if he knew her. I thought his reaction had something to do with the rumors, so I ended our conversation quickly, and went about my business.

Barbara pulled off her mittens, carefully stacking them on her lap. Sitting up, she clutched at her layered housecoats, adjusting them, wrapping them tightly around her slender white neck. I noted she had on at least two sweaters under what appeared to be three robes. Her foot peeped out from under the blankets as she straightened up. It was covered with several pairs of men's socks.

She reached for the mug of tea with both hands, bowing right into the steam. A cloud of vapor covered her entire face temporarily. She sniffed loudly, then took several large gulps before looking up. Our eyes met for the first time.

"I'm so sorry" she whined as tears suddenly oozed through her long lashes.

"No real harm done," I replied, "Not to the babies, I mean. Thank God. But, what about you?"

I watched as another violent tremor ran through her body. She tried to control her hands, but some tea splashed, hitting the stacked mittens. I reached out and took her hands, cup, and all, and said, "Exactly how long have you been an alcoholic?" She had 'bottomed out' holding one of my babies, after only three days on the job.

Pentti Junni

THE FIREFLY

The firefly – so mysterious –
I seldom see its light;
it only blinks its tiny lamp
in the heat of the summer night.

In a dusky cloak of velvet
Mother Nature robes the land –
but soon the dark is pierced by
the firefly's burning brand.

Its lover cannot hear the sound
of this lovecall in the night;
but comes when it is beckoned
by the tiny signal light.

To everything around us
Mother Nature puts her stamp –
even the little firefly
that roams the night with its lamp.

We can gaze in awe and wonder
at Nature's wondrous sights;
and wait, like the little firefly,
for sultry summer nights.

Translated by Kaarina Brooks

WOOD ANEMONES OF KARELIA

The hills of my mind are fragrant
with wood anemones white;
they cover the downs in springtime
whenever my fancies take flight.

The pure white, delicate blossoms
on a distant Karelian plain,
the stalks so green and slender,
in my memories they remain.

Those burgeoning hills of Karelia,
to me they are forever dear;
Though I never again may go there,
in my reverie they are so near.

If I could fulfil my wishes
when I dream of the flowers once more,
I would bring them all home and plant them
in my garden – for me to adore!

Translated by Kaarina Brooks

Diane Jarvenpa

DANCE LESSON

You walk me backwards,
step one two three and four.
You grip my hands hard as if preventing me
from falling over some great precipice.
We stop breathing as we collide into other bodies,
the rhythm we are trying to map and retrace again
tumbling and rolling away from our feet.
It is New Year's Eve and we are scuffing our shoes
across the linoleum floor of the Danish Hall.
We are learning how to tango.
The social worker from the Veteran's hospital
says it is simple, just walk, guide your partner,
let your pelvises meet.
Looking at this group, the meeting of pelvises
is not a customary public endeavor.
It is simple he says again. Just walk. Now rock, now dip.
But it isn't simple. We know what simple is.
Simple is hanging up on those ardent telemarketers,
letting the dental technician scrape your gums.
You step on my feet. I step on yours.
We turn in opposite directions.
The band plays Finnish tangos,
songs about sea birds, lost chances, harbor roses,
all the while the dance floor is cluttered with
tripping feet, couples lunging and lurching
like scores of giant carp snagged on fishing line.
I hear something in the far off distance,
most likely the whole nation of Argentina throwing back
it's perfectly postured head and howling.
We try again. You unclamp my hands,
I follow your steps, we sweep past the pot luck table
groaning with unearthly concoctions.
Something is happening, passing over the same footprints,

the pattern worn smooth, our feet no longer seem to be wading
stiffly through an Arkansas mud bath,
our bodies no longer orphans of dank basements
and work cubicles with static-ridden telephones.

We have crossed over to the other world.
Dancing like Neruda's butterflies,
"a dance that is...blue, white, garnet, yellow and violet."
This is a country village and it is the grape harvest,
this is the night of the northern lights
and the reindeer are racing down the city streets,
this is the festival of the pearl divers,
lanterns and fireworks bloom a thousand coins into the sky.
The music ends and we let go.
We are lined up around the room like the new apostles,
some of us shrug and get a cup of coffee,
some of us fill plates with hard tack and Havarti,
some of us sing in silent praise of our bodies
that proved to be taut and light as tambourines.
We will not preach for we have not the language
but we will carry in the stony field of our body's memory
the way the room pulsed, lifting the clouds to reveal the moon
big as an African drum and shimmering like abalone,
this dance born in the slums of Buenos Aires
and outlawed by the Pope,
born again in a Danish Hall in south Minneapolis,
taken to our flesh and pronounced into the quiet
dark morning of a new year.

Marlene Ekola Gerberick

TO A TREE, ROOTED IN GRANITE

In your wedding photo, faded
from fifty years of seeing,
your eyes tell
of carrying to the altar
the seed of a drunken, womanizing,
joyous, hair-lipped Frenchman.

You, Nordic, twice as tall,
bearing your punishment within,
went from the Lutheran altar
where hardship was worshipped.
Went to the rock filled farm,
struggled the soil,
worried the winters,
entered labor's bed to bring forth
nine times,
then he left

you alone
with your seeds,
struggling,
grew tough like the hemlock.

Winters came,
still you stayed.
Cold winds howled your limbs
but you were rooted.

Give me no tales
of Mary or Martha, Esther or Ruth
I know you

my strength increases.

THE ANCIENT FINN, FAR IN THE NORTH

Dark pines
sighing day and day; melancholia of trees and wind
forests inhabited by spirits only
nothing alive but him

and he just barely.

In the barn are ghosts of his wife and brother.
He goes there to talk with them.
Rages, finally,
because they won't live in the house with him

ever again.

His dog recently died, no longer lies sickly by the stove.
Now comes whenever called.
The dog's eyes are full of questions
which the old man cannot answer

doesn't even try.

His long ago children play in the fields.
One follows butterflies, another simply runs off.
He must always be in search of them.
He is so tired

can't find the children anywhere.

Somewhere he lost his teeth. Potatoes a failure this year.
He looks down the path, sees his wife,
puts his hat on his head (an old familiar gesture)
goes to meet her

but she turns; walks softly toward the barn.

THE SWAMP DOLL

It was early spring the day
I found that old doll
on the edge of the swamp.
Just one hand stuck up
out of moss and muck.
I pulled gently but long
until I had her freed.
I washed her off
in the irrigation ditch
dried her with bracken ferns
then walked a while
cradling her in my arms.

I sang old Finnish incantations.

When I got to Mrs. Clement's
back pasture
I saw a stump with ant tunnels.
It was a castle
but all askew
like maybe Gaudi had designed it.
I put her on the stump.
I put arbutus blossoms on her head
a rabbit's thigh bone in her hand
then turned and ran
as hard as I could until
I was deep in the aspen grove

where I knew she couldn't see me.

That was the reason we had
so many blueberries that summer.
Everyone else thought it might be
the plentiful rains
or the absence of late frost

but no, it was the swamp doll.

I went back, later, to that silver stump.
She was still there.
She was still holding the rabbit's
thigh bone in her hand.

FEAST DAY

Eino
whose fingers are soft and full and rounded
like goat's teats
whose stomach is a bloated balloon
which rests on his knees when he sits
and has more chins
than can reasonably be counted,

Eino
comes to make love to the mashed potatoes
romance the turkey
sing soft melodies to the rolls and butter
run his tongue caressingly over the pumpkin pie

then
he lifts his belly to the sofa and snores.

Eino's love is spent.

THE JOINING

In the eye of memory
they sit around the kitchen table.
It is always winter.

On the table
breads baked from grains my father
harvested, dried in the sauna,
coarsely ground by his stone.
Jams smelling
of brief, hot summer.
Cheese made from new milk,
pot after pot of coffee
thick from the boiling.

In this strange light
I look from face to face
and see we are becoming the same.
In the dusk of this winter afternoon
the light diminishes
and I become one with
Aunt Jenny, Uncle Victor, Uncle Heikki,
Uncle Eino, Aunt Hilja,
my father.
As long as I live, they live.

When I die, they are gone forever.

Kaarina Brooks

THE LAST WALTZ

(Nursing Home, 1995)

In the narrow space
between the bed and dresser
I dance with my father.
The tiny tape recorder on the windowsill
softly sings an old Finnish waltz:
*"Kauan katsoin
        sinua syvälle silmiin..."*

He gropes for the lyrics,
        never quite
        catching
        them.

I gently rock the wheelchair from behind,
        or dance before him
        holding his parched hands.
The vacuous smile indicates his pleasure.

As I sway slowly with his arms,
  the smile mutates into a leer,
  and, with palsied hands,
        he gropes for my breasts.

ELVI

Tragedy of Alzheimer

Elvi, vibrant poet maiden,
Tells of her ancestral homeland,
Sings in long and loving lyrics,
Weaves a tale in words and music.

Kalevala's dancing daughter,
Mischievous dark tresses tangled,
Sings the praises of her people,
Celebrates with zestful rhythms.

Somewhere, inside that empty stare
whimpers the dying echo
            of her song.

FINLAND, MAY DAY, 1939

I can only guess how they are feeling,
the nine young people in the photograph -
      tiny, black and white,
      in mother's tattered album,
      tied with brown silk tassels.

My parents (almost married then)
with others I don't recognize,
precariously perched upon the parapet
      of the old tower of Puijo,
      on the highest hill of Kuopio,
      above the maze of lakes and forests
      and their homes.

So drunk with joy and love are they!
Dying to soar off that wall
and dive reckless, headfirst, into life!

Their world is not black and white
but blushing with hues of spring
and loud with tones of youth:
      the girls demurely smiling,
      the lads cheering lustily,
      one's arm around his lady love,
      another's fist raised up in mock defiance!

They do not know that when November comes
they will be called to take up arms and die.

      Or perhaps they know...
      and that's why now are
      celebrating life!

NORTHERN LIGHTS

Walking home in boreal chill,
    in rub-your-cheeks-with-snow cold,
    skates thump against our shoulders.
Our breath hangs before us in a frozen cloud.
We stare at the black night sky, craning our necks,
    parka hoods thrown back for better viewing.
The seven stars of the Big Dipper pierce the darkness.

    Then – "Oh, look! Look!"
    Two pale green shafts of light
        rise from the west!
    And as we gaze they grow... swell....
    Two tall beacons, wildly undulating
        flare up past the zenith!
    They shrink to nothingness.

    Then suddenly the northern sky
        is ablaze with burning pillars!
    Pink... green... white!
    Lofty columns - cool and flaming
        flow eastward in exalted revelry!
    "Spirits of the dead, dancing before the Manitou,"
        says Sylvia, my Ojibwa friend.)
    They wax and wane... flare and flicker....
    So many blazing pilasters!
    And all the while the stars shine through
        behind them.

We didn't know – in that northern village -
    of great cathedrals
    or majestic organpipes.
But the phosphorescent stanchions -
    luminous and swaying,
    gloriously star-bejeweled -
        awed us to silent reverence.

    Forty years later, in Cologne Cathedral,
        I remember.

IN MY GARDEN SWING

Late summer's drowsy rays caress my arms;
the wearied book lies open on my lap.
My father's memory lingers by my side,
as gently, gently sways my garden swing.

The hummingbird thrusts down its slender beak
to sip last drops of nectar from the bloom,
rhythmically nodding up and down,
as gently, gently sways my garden swing.

The tall pink hollyhocks stir soothingly
in ripe, ambrosial breath of summer's end;
from side to side – and tremble languidly -
as gently, gently sways my garden swing.

The trees above shed dusky silhouettes
that slowly dance upon my upturned face;
rock back and forth like silent pendulums,
as gently, gently sways my garden swing.

The season slows its steps to funeral pace;
the mellow bees crawl, droning, in and out
of large and drooping white hibiscus blooms,
as gently, gently sways my garden swing.

The sated summer soon will lie asleep...
then wake to April's happy roundelay.
My father slumbers, cradled by the stars...
yet gently, gently sways his garden swing.

Susan Vickberg-Friend

VULNERABLE

like standing on a transparent floor
naked
or suspended inside a sphere of glass
untethered
visible to all who stare inside
a specimen

around me they speak and inspect
my voice resonates back to my ears
alone and labeled
"do not bend, fold, staple or mutilate"

DIAGNOSIS

i wait
i cry
i cry
i wait
for the pathology report
can it be repaired or not
i wait
i cry
i wait
i hope

EXCISING

My lips
Hear no words.
There are no visions
In my ear.
The surgeon works
My body thankful shouting:
"Be gone Devil!! Cancerous disease."
The open hole now stitched up.
Crafted as a quilt;
The artistry
Left upon my face.

Ernest Hekkanen

THE LAST RITES HOTEL

Here in the dark of the Last Rites Hotel
doors swing askew on hinges,
keeping time to the rock of bedsprings
where joy is had for quarters, even pennies.

Hotplates perform daily miracles,
and everywhere grease is rife.
There is the bottle which will hold off
the night. There is the crack in ceiling plaster
where despair seeps through like a stain.

I have had my fill of spuds and gravy,
I have drunk the red glow down into my guts,
and now I am back in the streets,
holding firm my course in the jostle and sway.

What I want is a fair day, and no more
voyages on the Polar Bear which breaks the ice.
I want embraces which will never let me go,
and to wag until my sorrow's wagged out.

But what I am left with is this: a souvenir
from the Isle of Man, one that ripples
like sail or scar on the sea of my heart.

109

A SANCTUARY OF SMELL

Today I am seeking sanctuary
in the Carnegie Library.
Trembling legs ascend
a spiral of granite steps
hollowed out by so much two-way traffic,
the unwary could sprain an ankle.

I don't read anymore.
I pull books down from shelves,
cracking them open one by one,
drawing the scent deep into lungs.
I breathe in printer's ink, must,
fingerprints left by persons unknown,
glue crystallizing along spines,
words decaying in half-lives
on pages so fragile
they resemble dried flowers.

Yes, dried flowers; that's what I'm reminded of:
dried flowers kept in an alabaster pitcher,
one with a neck as graceful as a swan's.
I'm reminded of how my mother
used a paint brush
to paint dust off mummified petals,
each pass of the bunched hairs
exposing faded colors to sunlight;
and I'm reminded of the scent
given off by cloak and flesh –
a kind of poem floating warmly on air.

No matter which streets I tread,
no matter how far I am from home
(little more than a mirage now)
I can visit my mother in this manner.
I can watch her paint petals
free of dust,
and now and then if I am fortunate,
I can hear her utter several phrases
in a voice cracking of parchment.

No, I do not read books anymore.
I breathe them in one by one,
and instantly they comply by telling me
everything I need to know.

REACHING FOR WORDS

Today reaching for words is like reaching
for sunlight. I would like to contort my way
out of this darkness, with a phrase so incandescent
it would make me feel immaterial, if only for a moment.

I would like to polish myself until I'm so bright
I would illuminate every dark corner of this city.
I would like to shine from one side through to the other,
like the most faultless crystal imaginable.

But today I can't find the words that ignite.
I can't see through this cloying opaqueness
which the sun flutters against like a dying moth;
and my mind, God help me, is like cold, dense clay.

VIEW OF THE HINTERLANDS

The pre-dawn hours between four and six
have become sacred to me. That is when
I go wandering in the landscape of my psyche.
That is when I head out along parapets
overlooking dark, steaming hinterlands
arrayed like backdrops in ancient paintings.

I find a place in myself to sit and watch
the sun rise over the distant, foaming sea.
I am alone on this promontory,
in this utterly speechless landscape,
a chill crawling up my spine,
accessible to the first morning rays,
and there I wait for the remarkable to come.

STRAYING FROM LUMINOSITY

My life has been one of straying from luminosity
and back again. My waywardness has led me
across steppes so vast I have wondered if
they would ever end. I have found this world
so alluring I have braved the bardo of becoming
countless times, simply so I could wallow in the delight
of wearing flesh. I have become so dense with longing
for rivers, mountains, plains and valleys
I have taken the form of every breathing thing.

There is nothing I haven't done to come back here.
I have followed the scent of various perfumes.
I have been so lonely for human touch
I have surrounded myself by successive wombs.
I have craved the breast so badly I have nursed myself
back into existence. I have been so desirous
of sight I have gone blind with seeing. I have spent
innumerable lifetimes trying to acquaint myself
with light, only for it to elude me in the eclipsing dark.

I WAS AS LIGHT IS

In flesh once bright with longing
I moved through the world,
as certain as light is of pushing away
darkness. Nothing was impossible.
I was so bright with certainty
there was no room for the opposite.
My mind was prismatic;
light angled through it,
producing an array of colorful words
which formed the loveliest of paintings.
I strode in brilliance like a rainbow,
with flowing mane that glinted.
I fed upon rarefied meals
consisting entirely of photons.
I shone so fiercely in everything
I had to avoid reflecting surfaces
for fear of blinding myself.
I was as light is.

Now my incandescent flesh
is no longer so luminous.
When I travel through darkness
I leave behind shreds of light
like a wayward comet.
I have lost
so much of my former brilliance
I only dimly light my way.
During nights that lengthen
at the speed of sorrow,
I experience trepidation.
Shadows take enormous bites
out of me. I no longer move
with the certainty of light.
In winter when the sun
is a mere suggestion

on the southern horizon,
I long for summers
that once went on forever.
I no longer burn so warmly.
I wear sweaters most of the time.
The prism that was once my mind
angles light less efficiently now.
There is no longer any yellow
or violet
in my spectrum.
When I'm alone in a room,
I tend to doubt.
My mane no longer glints.
My words no longer dazzle.
I shine so feebly now,
I have to avoid reflecting surfaces
for fear of not seeing myself.
I am as darkness is.

BURT RAIRAMO

ANITA

She paused,
she began to ponder.
What was said?

The words were whisked
into the air
in abandon,
it seemed?

She paused to think
for the briefest moment.

The truth flew
searching its colors
through the skies
of the pondered pause.

A STRING.

Alas!
A string broke,
The weight of my finger!
A faulty string? Was it a word?

Can the string be repaired?
Replaced?
Will the Kantele sing again?

Will the Kantele be abandoned,
another take its place?

Will you say
"I didn't like you after all"?

The joy!
The string is repaired.
The Kantele sings again!

But alas!
It doesn't sound as sweet!
The memory of the broken spring
Lingers.

TREASURES.

I bet my mind
can equal or exceed
the sway of palm trees,

colors of autumn maples,
sight of thousand lakes.

I don't need
to travel near or far.

I just close my eyes.
There, there they are.

The beauty and the wonders
of my mind.

And there I open
treasures locked.

And they equal nature
in their thought.

After all isn't nature,
in me and me?

And the creator's key,
locked deep in me.

I pray, use the key
and give me the key
to keep.

Paula Erkkila

COSMIC BLISS

"Faust, taking his seat beside Helena."

"Thus hath success both thee and me attended,
Now let the past be past, behind us flung;
Oh, feel thyself from highest god descended,
Thou of the primal world whence thou art sprung!
Thee shall no fortress keep in hiding!
Still in eternal youth, stands, as it stood,
A wide domain for us, for blissful biding,
Arcadia in Sparta's neighbourhood!
Enticed to dwelling in this blessed harbour,
Hast fled into the brightest!
Now let our thrones become an arbour,
Arcadian be our bliss and free!"

From **Faust by Goethe**

1.

Venus was conjunction moon in the constellation of Aquarius. The date was June 24, 1972. Electrifying influences permeated the air and energ-ized the nearby forest, as Susan Swanson excitedly took her first steps upon European soil, in the Duchy of Luxembourg.

As far as she was concerned, these were her first steps in this life-time. She had been here before, in her most recent past life. She had resurrected like a phoenix, out of the ash-heaps and corpse-holes of the holocaust.

She once met a petite, friendly female rabbi from Persia at a Kab-balah retreat in northern California. When asked what brought her there, she revealed, in a hesitant, embarrassed manner, that she had once been a child victim of the holocaust. The clairvoyant rabbi immediately confirmed that she had been nine years old at the time.

Susan had flashbacks of standing under some open-air, pillared columns with a roof over them. She recalled barbed wire nearby. Some time later, she had a nightmare of being pursued on a hillside by a Nazi soldier, who shot her. The rest of that short life was buried deep in the recesses of her unconscious. She wondered if Rainer Maria Rilke would have considered her one of his early dead, angelic children.

Whether or not it was true, it was a part of her. She considered the Jewish child her middle self, according to the teachings of the Hawaiian Kahunas. She felt it was her responsibility to nurture that part of herself, in order to fully flower as a person in this lifetime.

Susan found herself, on this Midsummer's Day, under the extraterrestrial influence of the goddess of love and the ruler of emotions. She had been drawn more than 5,000 miles, toward the magical origin of her current destination.

She was headed for Suomi, land of suot or swamps. Most people knew it as Finland. It was the birthplace of her mother and father. It was the spawning ground for generations of her ancestors. She once read that the Roman Tacitus described Finland, the land of the Fenns, as the land of magicians.

Unbeknownst to Susan, Finland was to become her greatest love, the land of her heart's deepest tears and joys. She would find it to be a land of summer's hay and midnight days, filled with fresh air after the rain. She would soon experience Finland's somber fall initiation into solemnity, and crisp, cold winter's sharp clarity. After that, spring's burgeoning hope and aspirations were waiting for her, in that forest and lake-filled land of her ancestors.

Susan was young and 28, and had abruptly reached a critical turning point, the end of four cycles of seven, and the beginning of the fifth. It was time to start laying the foundation for the next ten years of her life. She had reached an impasse, until Andy, her elderly astrologer friend, recommended she explore her roots.

The company she worked for as a chemist transferred to another state, and she was left in a limbo with a modest-sized severance pay. Moving back to the monotonous Midwestern state she was born and raised in was not the direction she was headed toward. She was spoiled by the multi-cultural diversity of California. Unfortunately, there was so much going on, that she was getting overwhelmed by the richness of it all. She was aware a part of herself was missing. This

121

stopped her from being fully able to absorb and enjoy life's experiences. She frequently felt dissociated.

She was suddenly confronted with a jolting question. "What's next in this adventure of living?"

The answer seemed to come out of nowhere, so it seemed. Yet she knew that the same nowhere, that factor X of existence, feeds our very souls, or is shut out by the pressures of our mundane affairs.

Susan frequently felt she had been going along in life, like a soulless-looking puppet of a zombie, moved by the moon-filled tides.

Something was stirring up inside of her. Her unconscious was breathing a spark of new life into her being, and her body, mind, and spirit were responding, as if an instantaneous small death and rebirth were occurring.

The answer unexpectedly resounded from her lips, "I'm going to Finland!" She abruptly announced to her surprised husband.

There was no question it was the right thing to do. Their marriage was lost in a stalemate of arguments, but even her husband, in his drugged state of mind, could hear destiny's call. He gave his approval, as he angrily threw her hastily-assembled luggage and boxes down the apartment stairway. Susan catapulted out the door, indignant at the brusque sendoff, but determined to journey onwards. She was filled with a new resolve to search into the roots of her being.

After hitchhiking across the United States, Susan flew over the Atlantic on a cheap $212 round trip ticket from New York to Luxem-bourg. She had always prided herself on getting a good deal. She figured this came from her mother, who managed their meager money very prudently. Her mother, who starved and begged for food in her teenage years, bargained her way through life.

Her father had crossed the Atlantic in the opposite direction sixty nine years before she did. First he took a leaky boat, the Polaris, from Hanko, Finland to Hull, England. Then he transferred over to the Merion for the long journey of several weeks to Boston. The trip cost him $23 in 1903.

He followed in the footsteps of his father and uncles, who were draft-dodgers from the Russian czar. They were also seeking better opportunities, since their family of twelve children couldn't all stay on and manage the family farm.

Fifty years earlier, her mother sailed across on the White Star Lines' Homeric to New York. Susan's grandmother wanted her mother to earn some money in America, and return to Finland to further her education.

Her grandmother begged and borrowed to come up with the $118 the boat ride cost in 1922.

Opportunities in Finland looked very grim for Susan's mother, who was scorned for being a commie brat. Susan's grandparents were black-listed during the ugly aftermath of the 1918 Finnish Civil War, known as the white terror.

The roaring twenties in Massachusetts, and the meeting with Susan's dad in a woolen mill diverted her mother from her grand-mother's carefully-laid out course.

Now Susan, who had completed college in America, was returning for her mother, to discover how to further fulfill the hopes and visions of her village healer grandmother.

Although she had never known her grandmother, who died in 1924, she had been primed from a very young age to follow in her footsteps. She felt the ghost of her grandmother was pulling her with invisible strings.

There were occasional times she actually felt her grandmother's presence hovering above her. She figured her grandmother must have been a romantic, because one of those times occurred during an intense romance that started on a hillside of green manicured grass on her college campus.

2.

A taxi took Susan, along with her motley luggage, from the Luxembourg airport to the stately formal aristocratic setting of the town. The peasant and the hippie in her were stifled by the orderliness of the place. She quickly made an exit to the freedom of the verdant countryside, where she could refresh her breath, with the comforting vapors of the earth and its foliage.

After a brief and uneventful ride with a friendly driver, she found herself with scattered parcels on the side of a roadway. She stood there for a long time, in a narrow green-foliaged valley, reminiscent of Pennsylvania. She was somewhere south of the city of Cologne.

Suddenly Susan was seized by a vivid impression. Her whole being was infiltrated by an invisible memory cloud of inflated Nazi glory and German grandiosity. Twenty seven years after the war's end, remnants of a Rupert Sheldrake-like morphic resonance, lingered on in that valley to haunt her.

Susan acutely sensed a disturbing archetype of a people, who had broken through the gates of a long repression, gotten carried away, and soared too high. It reminded her of Icarus, who flew too close to the sun. His smaller feathers, which were held together by beeswax, melted in the heat, causing him to fall and drown.

She recalled the German writer Goethe had once suggested there was a 2,000 year cycle of the return of the repressed. She started speculating, as she was prone to do, that the German barbarian tribes beyond the Rhine, were finally taking out their revenge upon Caesar's legions.

Unfortunately, the innocent descendants of the Jewish souls, who followed in Caesar's footsteps, took the brunt of the onslaught of this perverted and murderous vengeance that fed the pumped-up Nazi haughtiness.

A wave of depression and sadness crept over her and struck a deep chord within. Her analytical mind became submerged under the painful weight of her unconscious repressed memories. Susan mysteriously transformed into a helpless and abandoned Jewish orphan, standing there with her various size boxes, bags, and suitcases, tied together with ropes. She became extremely vulnerable and fragile. If someone didn't come by to rescue her, there's no telling what might have happened.

She managed to attract the attention of a young, kindly, energetic, and enthusiastic furniture factory owner. He drove her into Cologne, to an old stark-looking stone building, inside of which was his sparsely-furnished apartment.

It was so scantily furnished, she wondered if it had been stripped of its contents, as had often occurred in the days of the Nazi home invasions. She began to panic. She wasn't sure if she was experiencing a flashback to her former life, or if she was being transported back in time. Could she really trust these Germans?

Susan was introduced to her rescuer's wife, who was a plain, thin, stern-faced woman, who wore old, thick, granny glasses. Her cold outward appearance belied her inward kindliness. She busied herself dutifully mothering Susan and providing her with nourishment. Susan began to feel more relaxed.

She had an uncanny knack for eliciting maternal instincts, even from the most unlikely quarters. The highlight of her hostess' culinary offerings were the boiled eggs, which she proudly displayed on the breakfast table the following morning.

Susan woke up feeling weighed down by the excessive belongings she had so hastily assembled back in Berkeley, California the week before. Bags and boxes were in disarray, with some of the questionable contents threatening to spill out. There were old clothes she would probably never wear again. Most people would have considered them to be rags. There were rocks and bones and other mementos. There were books she had lugged around for years, but not yet read. She hoped they might be influencing her through osmosis, and eventually fit into her grand designs. There were letters and papers that seemed important, but the significance of them had not yet been determined.

Susan had always been a pack rat, clinging onto seemingly useless items, dragging them along with her, like a security blanket. From afar, her collection of objects resembled the scattered bits and pieces of a collage of existences, held together as mysteriously as a slime mold colony.

She prided herself in not being one of those obsessively neat people, who don't accumulate things. She envisioned them as spending inordinate amounts of time keeping things clean, and suppressing all influences. She didn't want to end up living like them, in an empty and lackluster prison.

There were many times, however, that she felt she had an albatross around her neck. Perhaps, she was in her own kind of prison. She feared she would turn out to be a bag-lady or some other such eccentric. She worried she could end up aimlessly pushing around a shopping cart, full of hoarded items, that would never find a purpose.

Common sense dictated, she could no longer carry her load, and continue to travel in the carefree and adventurous manner which suited her. She tried to convey to her gracious hosts that she needed to consolidate her belongings and ship them off to Finland. She became extremely frustrated over her inability to find the word for cardboard box in her English-German dictionary. After a taxing morning for her and her German hosts, she managed to procure a sleeping bag in a Cologne department store. They drove her to a post office, and helped her to pack the bulk of her precious junk.

Finally, she felt free to resume her odyssey.

3.

Unencumbered now, and revivified, Susan lapsed into a delicious reverie, entertaining the prospect of some romantic interlude, portended by the Venus moon conjunction. Back out on the road again, her spirits soared. She stuck out her thumb, ready for whatever was to come next.

The afternoon found her racing up the German autobahn, in the company of a dark-haired businessman in his late thirties. He was pushing his speedometer up past 180 kilometers per hour. She quickly calculated that they were going close to 120 miles per hour.

There was something about this man's vibes she didn't like. She pretended to feign indifference to his recklessness, by turning her head the other way and looking unimpressed. It was hard to tell what his intentions were, but she pegged him for some kind of upstart. He certainly wasn't the Romeo she had been fantasizing about.

Luckily, due to the excessive speed, they soon arrived on the outskirts of Lubeck. She made some story up about meeting someone in the vicinity, not realizing that his lead foot would make it all possible. He reluctantly acceded to her request to be dropped off.

Relieved to be free of his repugnant influence, Susan breathed in the cool freshness of the early evening air, and wandered northwards along the roadside for several miles. Her heavy, framed backpack and attached sleeping bag didn't deter her. She still felt light and carefree.

Soon she excitedly spied a beach. She knew if she kept going around one corner after another, eventually she would find a surprise. She was an adventuress. Her seventy-nine-year-old astrologer friend, who was like a surrogate father to her, told her the best of her would come out on the road.

Her life to date had been a series of explorations and expeditions. Her former companions would tire out and fall back along the wayside, but she would keep forging onwards, around the next bend and onto the next adventure.

This was her first view of the Baltic. In the coolness and grayness of dusk, she surveyed an empty beach, strewn with giant German beach basket seats. The water was gray and slightly choppy.

So, here she was at last, on the shores of the cold and obscure waterway, that played a major role in the lives of the Balts, from whom she was partially descended. The Vikings traversed the sea to raid and conquer whomever they ran across. They marauded their way into Russia, and enslaved the inhabitants. They founded the Romanoff dynasty there.

The Finns and Estonians fished and hunted seals, and used these waters for commerce. It was also the sea for the Danes, the Germans, the Prussians, the Poles, the Latvians, the Lithuanians, the bee-keeping Livonians, and the Russians.

Realizing she would soon have to find some form of shelter for herself, Susan scanned the area to see if she could find some bushes to nestle under. There seemed to be too much development around, so she wandered over into a campground across from the cold concrete sea wall.

Her heart began to thump, as she entered a small kiosk, and discovered a most handsome specimen of a young man, well-built, tall to her liking, dark-haired, and dark-eyed and blessed with a warm and pleasant demeanor. Their eyes met in instant recognition of a bond, and they became transfixed with one another, from that moment on.

He spoke English. She nervously inquired, "Is there a place to sleep here?" The campground was full. "Perhaps you could direct me to some bushes nearby, where I could lay out my sleeping bag, that's all I need," she deceitfully stated with a sheepish grin on her face.

The mutual attraction was escalating, and he clumsily dropped something on the floor. He indicated he needed to close up and hurriedly finished his task, so he could continue on in this unexpected interlude with the strange and magnetic American woman, to whom he felt inextricably drawn. Her short, well-built frame, her long straight shiny brown hair, and her beaming smile pleased him very much.

He led Susan over to his white Volkswagen sedan, and instructed her to put her backpack and sleeping bag into the back seat. The car was already loaded with his belongings. They drove up the road a short distance, away from the park. He turned off on an isolated dirt road. Susan was besides herself with excitement, by the time he pulled over near some bushes, next to a hops field.

Looking upwards, Susan took in the magnificent white beams of the full moon. Venus sat brilliantly radiating her essence in conjunction with the moon. "*Willst du mit mir schlafen?*" she blurted out in her bold Ostrobothnian voice.

She was once told she was straightforward, like the Swedish girls, when it came to sexual matters. Clearly, however, in this case, it was not necessary to ask. He took her hand and held it for moment, silently giving his assent.

4.

It was predestined that the prince and princess of cups would finally unite. The air was filled with magic, and off in some higher realms, beyond the human ear, Goethe's chorus chanted:

"Who would think to blame our princess
If she grants the castle's lord
Friendly show of favor?
For confess, we all of us are
Captives, aye, as oft already
Since the infamous overthrow
Of Ilion and the agonizing'
Labyrinthian woeful journey."

Wolfgang, or Moppie, as he was affectionately called, and Susan stood together next to the hop's field. They were awestruck, as they stared at the splendor of the moon wedded to Venus in the constellation of Aquarius. This calmed and balanced them, so they were able to carry on the ritual of putting together a campground and a fire.

Susan soaked in the thrilling ambience of the earth and the sky. She marveled at the merging of reality and fantasy, and the opening into another world, beyond the mundane one we mostly find ourselves in.

Wolfgang pulled out a book containing some of the works of Goethe and Schiller. He greatly admired these two Renaissance men. He was writing his doctoral thesis on them.

He explained to his captive princess that Johann Wolfgang Goethe was the west's answer to the dilemma of individual freedom run amuck. He went on to say that his idol, Goethe, was a man, who spent his life weaving a tapestry, that blended feeling and reason into the harmonious personality of a practical humanist.

She wished she could blend the scattered fragments of her personality into some form of harmony. She had no idea that this German giant struggled so hard with his mind and emotions.

Wolfgang further expounded to his admiring-eyed American, that Goethe's friend, Frederic Schiller, was a Promethean. He constantly fought the battle between the ideal and reality, and expressed his painful Sisyphus-like struggle in his tragedies.

Susan had once read that Prometheus or Forethought was a clever Greek god, who molded man out of clay. He was constantly protecting man from the wrath of Zeus. He taught him many things, but there were always more human imperfections to be worked upon.

Susan could relate to Schiller's tragedies, since her own life had been overloaded with Pandora's miseries. But now, she was free to look at her life from another vantage point. Susan was very impressed by Wolfgang's intellect. She had never been so close to such an educated man before. Her own father, who was a concrete thinker, had

128

only gotten up to the sixth grade, and he didn't speak the best of English. Clearly, Wolfgang's English was far more sophisticated than that of her father's. She realized it was better than her own patchy grasp of the language.

As the ghosts of Goethe and Schiller joined them around the warmth of the fire, Susan began experiencing the beginnings of ecstasy. In the background, Susan's grandmother gave her blessings and approval.

Susan's dark, handsome Teuton delighted her with the soothing strains of a guitar ballad.

The ghost of Paracelsus hovered above, preparing to initiate them into the wondrous and rich mysteries of the harmony of the spheres, as it manifests on the earth plane.

They were about to tap into a rich vein of alchemical gold, the seed of which could bear fruit, could become pregnant with growth, at any time in the future of their lives, given the right conditions.

A sacred marriage was about to take place. Susan's inner male was to be awakened, and Wolfgang's inner female was to be revitalized.

Susan suddenly flash-backed to Andy's book-filled, ram-shackled cabin in the Santa Cruz mountains. He preached to her about Tantric sex and the energizing of the kundalini fire up the chakras. He urged her to read The Serpent Power, before she ventured off to Finland.

She had no idea, however, that it would ever happen to her. It had only seemed to be an abstract theory promoted by theosophists. She was about to discover the surprise of all surprises around the corner of her life's walks. The time was ripe.

5.

Wolfgang came to her and embraced her firmly. When their lips met, sparks flew. They unclothed themselves in rhythmic motion. Their bodies blended:

> "Near and nearer they're sitting now,
> Leaning one on the other,
> Shoulder to shoulder, knee to knee,
> Hand in hand, cradle they them
> Over the throne's
> Richly cushioned magnificence.
> Now no scruples has majesty
> In it's revealing
> All its intimate pleasures
> Thus before all the eyes of the people."

Susan first felt an electric buzzing sensation, hovering around the base of her spine, in the area of the muladhara chakra. Soon, the sensation moved into the second chakra, and all of her sex organs lit up with energy, and remained electrified for what seemed like an eternity. The energy spread throughout her entire chakra system. Her lotus chakra overflowed, merging with the energy of her partner, then merging with the earth.

She and Wolfgang had become conduits, through which the earth renewal rites were being channeled.

As they disengaged and slowly de-energized, Helena and Faust echoed in the background:

Helena. "I feel so far away and yet so near
And all too glad I say: Here am I! Here!"

Faust. "I scarcely breathe, words tremble, check their place;
It is a dream, vanished are time and place."

Helena. "I feel I'm lived-out sheer, and yet so new,
Blent with thee here, to thee, the unknown, true."

Faust. 'Prove not the dower of this rare destiny;
Though life's but an hour, our duty's still to be.'

Susan and Wolfgang snuggled up to each other, lying in their sleeping bags on their bed of earth. Her head rested peacefully in his arm. Their campfire slowly died with the night. They entered into a blissful sleep.

Mikko Mallinick

Poems from a collection called *The Human Condition The Human Condition*

I'll spend Wednesday listening to all the things
I missed because I was talking
I'll spend Wednesday watching every little thing
And when people ask me how Wednesday was,
I can show them and tell them.
I will say it was great.
I did justice to you, and I did justice to myself.
By the time I get home I'll be saturated with feelings
That won't allow time –
If I wrote down every amusing thing I heard,
If I took to heart everything in a day,
Your smile would remind me of cynicism thriving on
The wasted time talked

Protest this and protest that
relax man
Cleverly disguised time wasting life suckers
naked and outdated
Lazily taking up much too much space
Trendy small people looking for peace
Politically correct hangovers
Get a job.

Indecision's dark clouds rolled over the green hills of adoles-
cence
with nothing to offer but confusion and doubt
Soon the rain would fall

The many masks concealed the real
with nothing to offer but confusion and doubt
reversing, imploding and rewinding

Two old women who followed blindly came to my door
with nothing to offer but confusion and doubt
an organized faction of the apocalyptic enterprise

The problem is mine I think too much
with nothing to offer but confusion and doubt
unable to be one of – a simple people.

Wage earning power dispenser
Thank you so much for my new shoes
Enslaved by your salary, freed by poverty
Love's price is higher than guilt
And affection is 50% off
I will return this evening
Everyone has to eat
I've learned a lot from you
Still, my dreams are not for sale

My world is a fountain of disaster waiting to overflow
I keep checking my reflection 5 or 6 times a day
just in case
Flowing through the forest dancing with the shadows
I am the friendly river
and the ice on my shores melts when you look at me
watch what you say
I'm broken but I can be fixed
death is just a word like life and no-one gave me the handbook
for heaven
and someone misplaced life's rule book
say it again I like the ring of that
say it again I like watching the words roll off your tongue and fall
into my head
you are wrapped in you and I'm sidelined
by the fear that you
are the support underneath
the wall of confidence that helps me
communicate

A man jumped up onto the fountain's ledge
And looked toward the sky
Short and gray with a gun in his hand, and aggression in his eyes
Hands up for self pity – he screamed staring down the crowd
I replied that I felt sorry for myself in a voice not half as loud
The man cried out, please, be my friend and help me down from here
I started through the crowd of people
trembling, cold with fear
A gunshot rang out from behind my friend's back
he fell lifeless to the ground
Circumstances would not allow salvation to be found

Thought with no connection
Try listening to that day in and day out
Linkless people that leave you to fill in the blanks
In my school across the river without bridges
Ivy league book fanatics meet real people
listless trade destroyers
Lost at sea with nothing to save them but inflated egos.

PART FOUR:

(Re)Connecting with Finland

Bernhard Hillila

AT THE CAFÉ ENGEL, HELSINKI

I sit alone at a table for three,
a table scarcely a foot and a half square
but much larger in centimeters.
I look up from my "large coffee"
and my lingonberry tart, over
the fresh red rose in the bud vase, out
of the window of Café Engel --
yes, "Engel," not "Engels."
On the sculpted sign jutting from the wall,
I see the Café's *Engel*, its *Enkeli*,
its Angel, and one of her wings.

My eyes saunter beyond
to Senate Square, namesake of the nearby
Senate Building built in czarist times.
My thoughts detour
to the Parliament's current home --
Parliament House on Mannerheim Road --
but return to the Square
and its central statue of Alexander II,
labeled by Finns "the Good Czar"
of a Russia which often oppressed.
A bus unloads a Japanese tour group
to pose for photographs with Alexander.

Going to lunch or returning to work,
people cut across the Square
on cobblestones set in circles.
One derelict shuffles aimlessly past --
to be homeless in Finland takes effort
but evidently it can be done.
At 13 o'clock, a band of 20 players

whom I see but cannot hear
escorts the changing of the guard --
päävartionvahdinvaihto to the locals.

My eyes climb up hundreds of worn granite
stairs -- granite is close to the surface here --
to the gilt crosses and sun-washed statues
of Helsinki's neo-classical Great Church.
At the next table, a lady takes
a cell phone from her purse
to speak softly to a good friend
while waiting for her drink.
I place a cube of hard sugar in my mouth,
sip strong, hot coffee through it
and begin to write a letter to Esther.

SULO

(A Rondelet)

Deep furrowed lines
crease Sulo's brow, drawn there by genes --
deep furrowed lines
etched deeper still by grief's designs
and farmer's work since early teens.
Fields still are Sulo's favorite scenes --
deep furrowed lines.

GRANDFATHER EINO

Mäntyjärvi -- just one of Finland's 100,000 lakes --
embraces each of its dozen islands. It washes
the clean beach -- and the granite beside the beach.

Beside the lake, a modest sauna of pine logs
smokes its last pipe for that midsummer Saturday,
sends mini-clouds rising toward the high sky.
Through thin soil, the sauna's posts rest on granite.

Beside the sauna, a birch grows pine-high
toward a sky flying Finland's colors. In its bark,
it bears the names of Sulo and Onni, lads who left
it long ago. Its roots cling stubbornly to clefts
in the granite base just below the skin of the soil.

Grandfather Eino sits on a bench at the foot
of the birch beside the sauna and contemplates
the lake, smokes one last pipe for the day,
thinking of Sally, Tommy, Tiffany and Dan --
his grandchildren who grow in America. The old
soldier's will has been granite, but his heart is tender.

ON A ROLL

*Studies in Finland have shown
that one pat of Benecol three
times a day helps promote
healthful cholesterol.*

One Pat Benecol,
bless his soul,
was jammed on a bun
with sweet Cherry Jelly,
headed for Mäkinen's
cholesterol belly.
He said, to be droll,
"Cherry, Ma chérie,
we're on a roll!"

THE WAIST

I am so slim,
the waist for
an hour glass.
Now through
me, past me,
the pregnant
past presses,
squeezes.
Beyond
me
history
becomes
my mystery,
futures open.
My roots are
up above me,
my branches
reach down.
I am so small.

Mark B. Lapping

IN ESTONIAN WOODS

A gaze across the yard to the line of trees
sagging under the weight of a late winter snowstorm,
wet, heavy, both the pride and the conceit
of this time of the year.
A thought about those who feared this snow most;
it pulled them toward gravity, trudging through it
leaving tracks and paths easily followed.
Those who made of these woods their home, their
safety against the deportations, their staging-areas,
they must have hated this time most.
How could it not be so?
Wet, hungry, diseased, thirsty, tired beyond fatigue,
ever fearful of betrayal, capture, failed memory.
I have come back to reclaim this small compound of
broken and drafty buildings. Ancestral home. Yet I am
owned by it or, more accurately, by its spirits and moans,
cries of babies and children, broken men and women,
rotting potatoes, the acrid smell of slow death.
History catches up with and captures everything
in such a late winter snowstorm.

Pentti Junni

DEATH VALLEY

The name of the place: Death Valley,
brings premonitions of doom,
Though years have passed, the memory
of that day is filled with gloom.

The fight was for the freedom
of our precious northern land;
t'was brother against brother...
and I try to understand

how some of our erring brothers,
also wanted to give their all,
but deceived by a wrongful message
they heeded the enemy's call.

So many brave men of Finland
did not see the lurking threat
of the neighbour's giant shadow;
and some do not understand, yet....

The deciding battle was fought
in bloody Death Valley, where
they met on Rasuli Road;
the fighting was bitter there!

When the battle was over and silence
like a shroud lay over the plain,
so many of our brave clansmen

would never rise again.
The people who still remember
tell tales of those bitter fights:
how a sacrifice was given
for our freedom and our rights.

Two decades of peace: the people
had a chance to build once more.
But the flames of hate were rekindled -
and Karelia was lost in the war!

The victory went to the stronger,
but I'll never give up the dream
that someday the Giant Aggressor
will pay for its evil scheme.

"It was Hell there in Death Valley!"
the souls cry from beneath the sod.
One day it'll demand a sacrifice
of the Oppressor's blood.

* * *

(Time: Civil War, 1918
Place: On the Rasuli Road, in Rautu,
Karelian Isthmus)

Translated by Kaarina Brooks

"MONOLOGUE"
Summer, '92

A rose I pick from a bush at my old homestead and smell its fragrance – so familiar ... fragile.

Through the overgrown paths around the yard I wander. Time has stolen everything: the sound of lively voices, the bustle of work – everything that was so familiar then.

Deserted house, decaying walls – they cannot stand much longer...

The fields, blossoming with fireweed – beautiful and red, no longer remember the fragrance of flowering oats, remember the sight of a waving wheat field.

The old fir trees in the yard gave shelter from the winter winds so long ago, though they were smaller then. Now the proud giants reach their crowns to the heavens and likely don't remember a little boy from fifty years ago.

To the shore of the bay I wander where the point of land shimmers in the distance ... thick with summer cottages! Whose they are hardly concerns me. No doubt they are good, industrious people who take pleasure in the clear, light summer evenings in the country.

So be it...though it didn't have to be thus. Life has merely taken its own course, oblivious to those it might be wounding on its path. Let me accept it and cease these nostalgic musings.

The stinging pain is dulled by distance, for now I dwell beyond the great ocean. It is there that I now feel at home and those environs I long for.

Torn from my birthplace while still a child – transformed into an emigrant...

... that's what I am: a Karelian.

Translated by Kaarina Brooks

Mary Caraker

HOW TOIVO SAVED THE WORLD

Toivo Uusitalo sat motionless on the stone steps of the cathedral in Senate Square, afraid to disturb in any way his aching head. It was a typical summer morning in Helsinki, the sun appearing only fitfully from between banks of clouds, but still Toivo shaded his eyes against the faint glare reflecting off the cobblestones.

If only he hadn't downed those last two *Lapin Kultas* at the party last night! Why couldn't he have stopped when Kaisa had suggested he'd had enough?

"I had to show her," he muttered, groaning. Show her that he was no callow youth who couldn't hold his beer. Just as he'd had to show Arto Nieminen, his former partner at the tax office, that he was able to celebrate Arto's promotion with no ill feelings.

Of course, it was all pretense. How could he help being jealous? The promotion should have been his. He'd been there six months longer, even helped train the glib-tongued Arto. But who cared about seniority and punctuality and a neat desk when the other fellow had a smarmy, mannequin-handsome face and a repertoire of ready jokes? Toivo groaned again, reflecting on the disparity between himself and his rival. No, Toivo Uusitalo, with his hesitant manner, his forgettable features, his pale hair that stood up in wisps and tufts no matter how he combed it, his feeble excuse for a beard that failed to disguise his weak chin, was doomed to be forever passed over, a drudge who would never amount to anything. And after last night's fiasco, he'd probably even be shown the door by Kaisa.

Kaisa. Plump, cheerful, comforting Kaisa. In his misery, Toivo wondered as he often did why she had stuck with him for so long.

He had no difficulty answering his own question: his steady paycheck, of course. And there wouldn't even be that inducement much longer if he didn't bestir himself and drag himself off to work. He was already an hour late, and there was no way he cold sneak in without attracting the boss's attention.

The bells in the cathedral behind him chimed, as if reprimanding him for his tardiness. As he struggled gingerly to his feet, Toivo heard something clattering behind him, then winced as he felt a strong grip on his shoulder.

The wince became a cold shiver as he glanced sideways and then upwards. His accoster stood at least seven feet tall, and appeared to be a collection of upright, gray metal tubes or pipes, a construction with no discernible head. Suction pads on several of the lower tubes enabled whatever it was to stand, and those on an upper one to maintain its imprisoning hold.

Toivo would have collapsed if the creature had not continued to hold him upright. He would have thought the whole encounter a figment of his still disordered brain---a last revenge of the *Lapin Kulta*---if the grip on his shoulder had not been so painful.

Yes, it was real enough, there was no doubt of that, as the creature propelled him down the steps. A passerby on the square below glanced up curiously, but if anyone else noticed anything unusual they hid it well. For once Toivo silently cursed the phlegmatic nature of his countrymen, but he was too much like them, even in his extremity, to want to cry out and attract attention. And as the two slowly descended without further incident he was thankful he hadn't made a scene. The thing pushing him was probably a costumed advertisement of some kind. Indeed, the construct was vaguely familiar, though at the moment he couldn't place it, and the person within, with limited vision, only needed guidance down the dangerously steep steps.

First Speaker of the Ip-Elg tightened his grip on the earth creature. So far, everything had gone as planned. The green world, as reported by the scouts, was ripe for a quick and easy conquest. First Speaker had beamed safely from the hidden Ip-Elg ship and had materialized inside the temple. Though there had been no one there to approach with his instructions, the puny specimen seated outside seemed a docile enough messenger.

The soft-shelled creature uttered a squawk, and First Speaker reduced the pressure of his fore-limb. The two were now on a level surface, and there was no need to guard one's balance. It was time to communicate.

"Take me to your leader," First Speaker enunciated clearly, repeating the sentence in all six of the earth languages he had mastered.

Toivo stiffened in surprise at the garbled sounds that issued, hollow and tinny, from an aperture in one of the pipes. "What? What did you say?" he responded, feeling stupid to be talking to a collection of pipes,

147

and even stupider as he continued to be held captive by it.

The pipe creature gave Toivo a tooth-rattling shake and repeated, more loudly, its stream of sounds.

Only one phrase from the outpouring sounded vaguely familiar. "Take me toorlidder." Could it be English? Toivo was fairly fluent in the language, but he couldn't translate the last word. He repeated the phrase as he had heard it.

"Yis, yis," the creature said, shaking Toivo again. "Take me toor lidder."

Toor lidder. Toivo thought desperately. Of course---Tour leader! Foreign tours were always stopping at Senate Square, and the person inside the clumsy costume had probably gotten separated from his or her group. In fact, as Toivo glanced hopefully all around the periphery of the square, he spotted a blue and yellow tour bus pulling away at that very moment.

"Stop! Wait!" Toivo ran, the pipe construct clattering behind him, but the bus was gone before they reached the street. "I am sorry," he said in careful English to whoever it was inside the metallic tubes. "Perhaps you can join another tour. There should be another bus along soon, and they all take in the same sights." He tried to back away politely, but the creature seized him with four of its pipes (how did it manage that? Were there two people inside?) and bellowed so loudly that several passersby paused and stared. One of them even stopped talking for a few seconds on her cellular phone.

"Take me toor leader!" echoed from the pipe vent as Toivo was once more shaken unmercifully.

"Yes! Yes, I will," Toivo agreed hastily. Anything to pacify his tormentor. Anything to avoid making a public scene. Anything to stop having his hungover brains jiggled.

The creature released him. Toivo mouthed a silent prayer as he searched for another tour bus, but for once there was none in sight. "Take me---" came again from the pipe, even louder than before, and Toivo held up both hands in a gesture of surrender.

"Follow me," he said. "I'll be your tour leader." What else could he do? The creature wasn't about to let him go, and he was already so late to work, and in so much hot water, that another hour wouldn't make that much difference. Besides, he knew now why the collection of pipes looked so familiar---it had come to him in a flash of recognition---and he also knew where the costumed person or persons probably wanted to go.

148

Toivo and his companion boarded a city bus. Toivo cringed at the prospect of the attention they would surely attract, but only the small children among the riders had the discourtesy to stare and point. The adults, in true Finnish fashion, kept their eyes on their newspapers and their thighs careful inches from those of their seat partners. Toivo directed his companion to the rear of the bus, where they stood in silence until the stop at Sibelius Park.

Toivo helped the pipe creature down the bus steps and along a tree-lined path. "This must be what you wanted," he said as they came in sight of the towering silver monument.

Perhaps the pipe costume was a tourist promotion of some sort---maybe a celebration in honor of the great composer. Toivo didn't care what the ridiculous contraption did now, just as long as he was rid of it.

First Speaker stared, transfixed. A representation of two Elgs in the attitude of command, perfect in almost every detail. His thinking tube pulsed. How was it possible? The scouts had been disguised; no one here could have known their true appearance. But...there it was.

Speaker circled the monument, and as he counted the number of pipes in each standing form, his sense tubes sent pings of warning through his entire system. The representations were not Ip-Elgs at all! They were Ur-Elgs! The ancient and deadly enemies had beaten them again, and erected the monument as a warning.

First Speaker quavered in all his tubes. He had to return to the ship immediately---he hoped it wasn't already too late. No world was worth a battle with the Urs, not even this green jewel. He activated his transporter and closed his sense tubes for de-materialization.

Toivo turned once to look back as he hurried away, and the pipe person was nowhere in sight. He didn't notice a peculiar beam of light or a sudden darkening of the cloud cover directly overhead, he was so obsessed with getting to his office as quickly as possible. He'd try to forget the whole episode, it had been so embarrassing. The only thing about it in his favor was that no one would ever know.

Erika Pollari

TRAIN-RIDE

As a foreigner I have ridden
the silent trains of Finland:
Those midnight trains that
slip silently into little-town
stations, and then slip out again,
leaving a dazed person on the
platform.

There is an unassuming
tranquility that falls upon the
passengers in those midnight
trains.

I have seen the soldier boys
with buzz-cut heads thrown back
in slumber, their mouths forming nice
little pink 'o's that contrast with
the slightly purple circles underneath
their eyes. One dreams of a girl's neck.

And the careless drunks that smile
benevolently down at shocked
children as they saunter down the aisles.
I tell them I speak no Finnish and
they still sing their folk-songs with
gusto to my face.

Ahh, these train rides that go back and forth.
My aunt waits for me at the end of the line,
but for now these people are my family.

The girl across from me, with the spiked blue hair
and the little blue eyes moves her head back and forth to
the pulses of a tribal song, and then falls asleep,
dreaming of that summer at the cottage,
when she was eight,
and swam the length of the lake.

These trains shake silently
with many dreams:
of first dates and skiing,
and old war memories and forests,
and the soft breathing of children – suddenly interrupted by
the announcement. "Kokkola – in five minutes".

And sometimes the dreams
spill on to the platforms;
but are quickly rubbed away by
fists from tired eyes.

Karen Driscoll

CHILDREN AT LAST

In 1976 Ritva was expelled from the Finnish Communist Party.

"I didn't pay my dues," she shrugged in retrospect. "I guess money was more important to them than they admitted! They tout human rights and free speech yet expel someone who'd been faithful to the party line for more than five years. Free speech! Hardly! In 1979 a prize-winning Chinese film was banned from the Kuopio Film Festival to protest the Chinese government's arrest of student protesters. All Maoist book shops in Helsinki temporarily closed down. They were only depriving Finns of cultural education; I mean, the Chinese didn't suffer because we missed one of their films or went a month without reading Maoist proverbs!"

She gave a long reflective laugh, displaying her large, very polished teeth and the sparkle that came to in her eyes whenever her thinking led her to new understanding about the past.

She took a comb from her bag and neatened her thin blond hair. She kept it cropped (once, even completely shaved) for the sake of convenience. She looked unkempt, even after she put on a touch of lipstick. The layers of brightly-colored skirts and blouses, the scarves around her neck, waist, and head added girth to the bulk of her tall, heavy body. By the time she had given birth to two children, she spent muggy, Canadian summers at home in a bathing suit. When she was lying on the bed reading, her body seemed particularly large in comparison with the tiny paperback novel she was holding.

Ritva exuded a vivacious honesty and love of life that was rarely encountered on the Finnish landscape. Even her dreams expressed a worldliness that equally well-traveled comrades were not in touch with.

"I was at the border, coming back from Easter in Leningrad. I had bought several books on Russian weaving. The border guard told me I couldn't take them back into Finland because they were a state secret."

"I dreamed I was hitch-hiking in Russia. I waited for hours in Siberian cold for someone to pick me up. Finally a car stopped and it was

152

Brezhnev, with a wolf fur cap on, and with those eyebrows! He gave me a lift. I don't remember where I was going, but I had to get there in a hurry."

When she was established in Ottawa, she wrote film reviews for a communist newspaper, but stopped when she noticed that her name was not printed with them. "The editor told me that true communists sacrifice payment and personal recognition," she said, miffed, but hardly surprised. She decided to enter the children's book review circuit and collected hundreds of review copies. Only three reviews were published, with her name.

Ritva's biting intellect and infallible perspicacity, coupled with unusual wit, caught the attention of only a few, for only a few were able to appreciate the synthesis of such sharpened sensibilities.

From the point of view of the intelligentsia at the University of Helsinki, she was always a little bit "off the mark". Although widely read and able to study books in German, Russian, Swedish, English, her idiomatic usage was clumsy. The main criticism of her Master's thesis on children's films was the poor quality of written expression. Although it was mainly a compilation of every children's film ever made, she had to rewrite it three times before it was accepted.

Yet her unpolished style, the contaminant of innumerable attempts at speaking foreign languages or writing literary criticism and scholarly pieces, reversibly functioned as fertile soil wherever she managed to gain ground with a charmed audience. It really was quite amusing when she accidentally punned with words that revealed her extensive vocabulary: "He died of a brain hemorrhoid." Someone guffawed and muttered, "There were several who probably should have!"

She seemed to internalize a wall against the everyday way of saying little things; after eleven years in Canada she still pronounced Ottawa with a 'v' and answered the phone with a comrade's salutation of announcing oneself surname first: "Here's Lahti, Ritva."

Her mother died when she was a young girl and her only brother in a car accident when he was seventeen. She was left with her stepsister and stepmother, her paternal grandmother, and her father. Her grandmother lived alone in a cold, wood-heated cottage that sat upon land she did not own. Her father, an overweight, bovine, multilingual businessman, kept it no secret from Ritva that he had been supporting a lover for over a decade. Years later, upon receiving a letter from Simon saying that Ritva was having an affair with a Ukrainian immigrant, he wrote to his daughter telling her how stupid she was for letting Simon find out.

Heavily influenced by Gorky's *Mother* and other heroines of the Bolshevik Revolution whose dream was to enlighten the illiterate masses, Ritva married Erkki, an uneducated, drunken man who did what he was told as long as it wasn't too much work. Ritva guided him, but in the end, he was not educable.

Mornings, after she had left for work at Dawn Light (a party-funded, anti-alcohol youth organization), Erkki cleaned the cramped apartment; afternoons he read Jack London at the spotless kitchen table. After her brother was killed, Ritva desperately wanted a child. "I want my brother's soul to reenter the family. I can sense him clamoring to get back to life." But she did not conceive. Erkki, bored with his role as his wife's student and stud, decided to get a job. He found one as bottler at a beer company, but was fired within a month for drinking company produce on the sly. So he got a lover. She was a student nurse who lived next door. When Ritva came upon them in a restaurant, both drunk, the neighbor's eyes red from tears shed in a lovers' quarrel, she immediately went home and moved her belongings to another neighbor's.

Ritva was headstrong, like a plow, and instigated abrupt change. She reacted passionately and never looked back. She decisively dyed her casual cotton wedding dress brown, cut off two feet from the hem, made a belt from the yardage and wore the revamped outfit to work. Her ex-husband married the neighbor, but was divorced within two years because his young bride never trusted him out of her sight. Whenever she had the time to go to a parade or to the movies, Erkki couldn't be bothered because he had a hangover. Besides, his new wife was still in school and Erkki managed to find only one job, in a pea soup factory, where he lasted a week and a half. His stomach couldn't take it for lunch every day.

Before she met Simon, Ritva had a winter-long affair with a serious photographer who lived with his aged grandmother in a small apartment. The spring before she left Finland he committed suicide by laying his head in a gas oven.

In Canada two years later, she got a letter informing her that Erkki had died one night, drunk, by falling in front of a train at a station outside of Helsinki. Ritva laughed ironically because "Erkki was too stupid to commit suicide, or to stand up straight on a train platform."

Simon was her ticket out. He was on a year's sabbatical from Ottawa's zoological museum researching the similarities between the North American and European mink. His basic tenet involved the belief in the land bridge that once connected Europe and North America. Although he was fifty years old, twice Ritva's age, he had direction. And she needed direction. Simon knew he had enough already, but didn't mind more from a fresh source.

He had four grown children by a Spanish woman, Anna, to whom he had been paying alimony for years with uneasy resignation. Besides Anna, he was under the reign of his aged mother who had divorced her American husband and moved to Canada when Simon was three. She criticized not only Anna but her son's other three wives and any girl-friend she was able to meet. She noticed whether they wore proper girdles or underpants, how they cooked, carried themselves, conversed, and especially how they influenced her son. They were the cause of his permanent angst.

Bitterly Simon spoke of his childhood and his mother. He was her only child and, although she had retired in Florida and was middle-aged, he still was not free of her hold. In his early forties, however, he commenced a life-long search of every relative he could find, no matter how distant they were. By the time his and Anna's children were married, and his two children with Ritva were born, the family tree took up a whole wall in the bedroom. By that time he had a familial connection to Finland, a whole new branch in the complex web of marriages and reproductions.

Simon had a few tics. When excited, especially when recounting his endless history of passionate affairs to new female acquaintances and ex-lovers, Simon sniffed relentlessly, as though suffering from hay fever. Ritva was oblivious to this habit, and, after several disappointing and expensive failures with other, more conventional, more beautiful, more discriminating Finnish women, Simon won her.

Ritva sailed through the courtship, happily smoking cigarettes (putting the ashtray outside on the windowsill because it smelled up the room), blissfully reading the poetry of Pablo Neruda late into the night, and repeating how beautiful life was. The posters of Hemingway and Che Guevera kept their places on her walls. She and her new lover fenced jovially about Soviet youth in bed after making love. Ritva claimed that if western products ever reached that highly evolved population, they would certainly reject it in favor of a culture of intellect.

"When I visited my 15-year old cousin in Petroskoi, she had posters of famous authors on her walls, none of the American rock bands! Russian kids really care about their education, they are happy with their books. They don't need the garbage America's trying to foist on the rest of the world. A public bus is good enough for them; they don't need a car or a motorcycle."

"But if they could have what the West has, they'd take it in a minute," Simon always protested.

She would either extol the moral grounds of the Pioneer Youth or recount her trip through Palace of Culture when she was in Warsaw for two weeks with a group of Finnish students of journalism. "They have a socially healthy upbringing. The boys and girls learn crafts together, read and draw together. They don't get exposed to the stereotypical models of what boys and girls are supposed to be; they don't learn ballroom dancing until they are sixteen years old."

That is how Ritva would bring up her children, when she had them. She still hadn't met Simon's children.

When Simon's doctoral thesis was complete, he asked Ritva to marry him. She accepted, quit her job, and they flew to Ottawa. She wore her brown wedding dress at the small ceremony attended by his children and a flock of his ex-lovers, now friends.

Three of Simon's children, all in their twenties, still lived with him. His daughter, Janet, and Ritva's instant dislike for one another threw the equilibrium of the household off balance. The two boys went about their business, treating Ritva as an aunt, graciously accepting, but never wearing, the great, bulky, woolen vests and pullovers she ferociously knit them.

Ritva had always loved handiwork and made it a point to visit ethnographic exhibits wherever she traveled in Europe. Her transition to life in Ottawa sparked a fury of unprecedented woolen busy-work. She ordered pounds of wool yarn from New Brunswick and crocheted and knitted several "productions". These sets of clothing were defined by striped color combinations: there was a red production consisting of a pleated skirt, a cardigan, and leg warmers; a green production of skirt, a button vest, gloves and a hat; and a purple production, a skirt, long pullover vest, mittens and shawl. She laughed when others laughed at the excessiveness of her handiwork and she would tell them stories of knitting from her student days.

"I made some wool socks that were too big for anyone I knew. We were out drinking one night and I had them in my bag. On the way to the train station we walked by a passed-out drunk slumped in a telephone booth. He had nothing on his hands so I put the socks I knit on him as mittens!"

Mittens made without the guide of a written pattern turned out so large that she gave them away as onion bags for the kitchen.

She bought a full-sized rug loom and began weaving yards of rugs and carry-alls. She visited the local thrift shop for pounds and pounds of cotton garments which she would tear into strips for rag rugs. She knit and wove so much she couldn't give it away fast enough.

Simon's picture of Ritva changed in the Canadian environment. Now that she had no reason to ever speak Finnish and he no longer depended on her ability to do so, he mocked her English, as well as her handiwork and her cooking. He expected her to do the cooking, as his other wives and lovers had, but he and Ritva had opposing views on the value of food.

Simon liked to think of himself as a chef, yet was unable to improvise. He had to follow recipes to the letter. After toiling for many more hours than the results merited, he would sit down and sigh in self-deprecation, "If I could only *cook*!"

Once he quadrupled a beef liver and pea stew for a dinner party for his colleagues. He added four times of each ingredient, including the salt. The recipe called for one teaspoon. He realized his error when his dinner guests nearly spat out their first mouthfuls of liver. While the group creatively decided to rinse off their chunks of liver in warm water before eating it, Ritva devoured her helping and took a second helping, leaving the guests dumbstruck. She ate that way: quickly, without savor.

Her banquets, on the other hand, were bland. One autumn she bought a twenty-pound bag of carrots. For the next month every dish was mainly of carrots: carrot salads, carrot soufflés, carrot cakes and quiches, carrot juice, carrot soup, raw carrot sticks with carrot and onion dip.

"Man does not live to eat, but eats to live." This was the Finnish maxim she lived by. She laughed when Simon groaned as she served reheated carroty leftovers. "Man does not live to eat, but eats to live!" she repeated, long after the sack of carrots was eaten, for Simon groaned as she served every meal she ever cooked. The family never finished a plate of her food, so there was always enough left to reheat and serve as leftovers the next day. Simon began to lose weight and his nervous sniffing increased in frequency. The family reluctantly came to the table when dinner was ready.

Ritva didn't notice her husband's tics and insecurities, but sensed them. She began to exhibit emotional shifts which she attributed to being at home all day. Simon said that she was "moody" and accused her of constantly trying to upset the household. Ritva thought she'd like a child and complained that they never went to the movies. She knit and wove, even in the middle of the night.

Ottawa is a city of immigrants, and Ritva soon figured out that this was her circle. She didn't like Simon's work mates from the museum, not fully grasping that their avoidance of her stemmed from discomfort rather than dislike. She seemed oblivious to Simon's mockeries and insults muttered at get-togethers, but resented his embarrassed work mates' distance from her. She got a job at the Swedish embassy and read every volume, in the original, of *The Immigrants*. From then on, her social life had nothing to do with Simon's, limited as it was.

Despite Simon's wishes, she got pregnant. "She did it on purpose," Simon told a crowd around the coffee machine at the museum. "I told her to use contraception, but she didn't. Just what I need before my retirement!"

The child was a healthy girl who Simon adored and Ritva, before her first daughter's third year was over, resented and abused. Ritva rarely spoke to Marja, and when she did, it was always in Finnish, always short imperatives. Simon had struggled with French until he passed the state exam, making him eligible for the museum job. He had learned his favorite foreign-language phrase, "La mia casa e la tua casa," from his Spanish wife. Though he could not get a grasp on Finnish grammar or syntax, he learned basic verbs and nouns such as "Brush your teeth," "Shut up," "Eat your dinner," "Milk," and "Come here now."

He complained about Ritva's abuse not to protect the child, but whenever it suited his purposes. "She pulls Marja's hair when she brushes it and makes her cry. She hates her own daughter. When she changes her clothes or gives her a bath, she's rough with her. It's awful hearing that from the next room. She reminds me all the time that I can't learn Finnish, but she can't even learn to bring up her own daughter right."

His eldest daughter Janet left home to live with her fiancé and to go to dental hygiene school. Ritva got pregnant again, but had a miscarriage after five months. She delivered the fetus herself and brought it to the hospital. She stayed in bed for a week while Simon maintained the house, reminding her that she'd driven Janet away, and why did she want to bring another child into the world, to abuse it?

It was after this tragedy that Ritva developed an allergy to wool and, in a compensatory gesture, discovered herself to be a painter. She took art classes and was never discouraged when her teachers told her that her work was sloppy. She persisted, sitting on the couch for hours, sketching on drafting pads, painting in the basement after Marja was asleep. With her first grant, she purchased a computer, "to write more grants." Within a year, she had exhibited her work with other immigrants, and had processed several themes: "Eggs," "Children," and "Doors of Perception."

Simon was proud of his wife's work and after lauding her talents to his work mates mumbled, "I used to want to be an artist, too, but never got around to it, with all my kids to bring up."

After a period of exhibiting strictly with other Scandinavian immigrants, Ritva moved into the English circle. She became fascinated with male homosexuality and fancied that various women were attracted to her. It was during this period that she shaved her head. "Marja was in the bathroom watching me in front of the mirror, trimming my hair. I cut it shorter and shorter, until I picked up Simon's razor and started shaving it off. Marja shouted, 'Mommy is cutting off all of her hair!'" Ritva told this story at the cafe. Then she pulled the brightly colored scarf off her scalp for the other artists to see.

She was sure that one woman sculptor was a lesbian, and that after the unveiling, behaved in an outwardly "sexual manner" towards her. "Hannah treated me like I was nobody before my hair was gone. Now she touches my arm when she talks, and criticizes my work as she would a professional's!"

She met and fell in love with a renowned middle-aged Ottawa painter, Ian Claver, who smoked joints and was surrounded by twenty-year-old blond artists. He tantalized Ritva, who became obsessed by her frustrated physical attraction to him. She spent $800 of one of her grants to purchase one of his very small, abstract paintings that appeared to have been created from some paint left over on a pallet and she hung it in the kitchen. One of Simon's sons remarked one evening, "You're in love with Ian, aren't you?"

This was the first in a long series of infidelities Ritva threw herself into with all her volition; although she wasn't sleeping with Ian, his name was constantly on her lips, no matter the company or the place. She was in his and his circle's company at least five evenings a week. She ceased taking part in her household. When she finally felt sufficiently duped, she quit seeing him for good, having gleaned enough connections to nurture her reputation as a community artist. Simon never uttered a complaint.

Ritva joined a video film consortium and, with another woman artist, made a film about two female Canadian artists. Neither Simon, nor any other member of his family, went to the first showing. Although she still lived with her family, this marked the beginning of Ritva's separation from them.

When she was later involved with a Moroccan from Montreal, one of her friends asked her why she didn't move to Montreal with him. "I need Simon's financial support so I can be an artist." Simon's supervisor was hinting at Simon's early retirement.

Ritva's father phoned to say that his mother had been moved from her house into a hospice for the dying. Ritva took Marja to the village outside Helsinki for two months. She arranged an exhibition, visited her grandmother and her father's family, and had a brief affair with a married Bulgarian jazz musician she met at a club. When she returned to Ottawa, Simon's sons had moved out and she was pregnant. The second daughter, named Katrina, was probably Simon's for she looked much as Marja had when she was born.

Simon's mother, who had been living in Florida, had a heart attack, so he moved her, against her will, to Ottawa to occupy the second floor. The contention that arose from this arrangement made life unbearable for everyone. Although she was frail from the heart operation and a double radical mastectomy, she despised Ritva with superhuman strength, and in the following years managed to cleave the furrows of hostility even deeper. She told Simon how cruel Ritva was to Marja, how she never invited her downstairs to dinner, how she was using them for their money. When Ritva wasn't home, Simon listened to his mother, but he never invited her to join his family downstairs.

After Ritva had weaned Katrina, she and Simon talked about divorce for a while. Ritva wanted to take Katrina and for Simon to keep Marja, but Simon refused this arrangement. Talk of divorce was dropped and Ritva started seeing Leo, an Orthodox Ukrainian. Leo encouraged her to return to Finland. "It's only a matter of time," she said. Simon, who was preparing for an early retirement, finally reacted.

Ritva found the letter he wrote to her father on the computer screen. She continued to spend whole nights and weekends with Leo. Simon found his address and telephone number on the inside cover of one of his wife's sketch pads, and would phone Leo's apartment at three in the morning. When Leo answered the phone, Simon hung up. Ritva knew it was her husband calling, but didn't end the affair until her interest was sated. "An affair gets boring when it's based on sex alone," she told a confidante one evening at the cafe.

She rented a studio in an old Catholic school and painted a series of pictures based on her grandmother's childhood photo-graphs. Simon had retired and was nervous about the discrepancy between his pay-checks and his retirement income. Ritva was at home less and less and he tried to make the effect of her absence obvious through neglect.

The children caught colds frequently and seemed hesitant to shed them. When Ritva came home late, well after supper should have been served, the girls were still up, crying for their mother. Simon thrust Katrina into his wife's arms while Ritva herself was trying to gobble up some stew. The children had become pawns in their unhappy game. Ritva responded by falling ill herself, some-times for a week at a time. The family became familiar with these attacks and attributed them to foreign viral strains. "Mommy is sleeping. She has the flu, the kind that gets worse every day, instead of better."

When the girls were playing in another room, Ritva would say, in a fe-verish delirium, say how much she wanted to have sex. Simon would un-dress and get into bed with her. She would be asleep, most of the time.

Four days after Christmas Day, they had guests from the States, a family with one child whom Simon had met when he was at a zoology conference in Massachusetts several years earlier. Ritva enjoyed the wife, who was fascinated by her eccentricities and palaver, and had called ahead to tell her to bring a formal dress to wear to an artist's New Year's party. The party was by invitation only. Even Simon had not received an invitation, a point he would frequently make once the American guests arrived.

When they got there after the long drive from Connecticut, Ritva was in bed with a long-term flu. Marja and Simon explained many times how Mommy had been sleeping for four days and gave the history of the Christmas tree ornaments passed down in Simon's family for many generations. The kitchen was filthy. The sink was clogged up with un-eaten food and dirty dishes. Ritva got up at mealtime, ate and talked voraciously, then went back to bed. On New Year's Eve day, she got a phone call. "Sylvia," she informed her female guest, "the invitation to the New Year's party has been taken back. I may not bring a guest. Invitations are for the addressed only."

"Surely you wouldn't go to a party of people like that!" laughed the guest, appalled at the thought of such a closed society.

"And I must pay twenty dollars to enter and bring my own snacks and beverage!" laughed Ritva.

There were more phone calls throughout the day. Ritva got up to answer them, then went back to sleep. At suppertime, Ritva ate well,

161

standing up next to the table, laughing and talking. She went back to bed, leaving Simon, the two adult guests and the three children to play board games and listen to music on the stereo.

At eleven o'clock, Ritva got up, put on fresh clothing, and went to the party. Everyone was asleep by the time she got home, so no one knew what time it was. In the morning, the guests went into the kitchen for coffee before they headed south. Ritva and Simon were already up and dressed. "I had such a wonderful time! I danced and drank hot cider all night. I must have danced my virus away!" Her bed was even made up.

At the party she had confided to a male friend, before they made love in a bedroom, that she was pregnant. He had known her for three years and asked her, after she had said that she would not have an abortion, why she would have another child. "Because," she said with melancholy assuredness, "children are an affirmation of life."

PART FIVE:

Connecting with Finnish Writers

Translator Börje Vähämäki

WHAT IS THE OLD ONE TO DO?

By Fredrika Runeberg

Shall I sing?
What shall I sing?
Good night, good night.
I shall sing no more;
I shall fall asleep.
Good night!

Why should I sing, for whom should I sing?
With old age a silver hair or two already creeps into my
curls.
The old one shall not sing.
What is an old woman?
A mote in the eye,
a splinter in the foot.

How shall the old one bring joy?
She shall be silent, she shall disappear.
She brings the most delight
When seen or heard by no one.
Quiet, quiet, you are already getting silvery hairs, hide,
Clear out, no one needs to see you.
Good night, good night,
I want to sleep.

Why does even the old one have feelings,
Why does even she want to live,
Why does she want to look beyond her own door?
Sleep, sleep, good night,
I want to sleep.
Quiet!

From behind the wall she hears cheerful speech,
from there she hears merry laughter.
It is the young men conversing spiritedly
About life's great dreams and about beauty.
The old woman is not to go there to disturb their joy.
Good night, good night,
I want to sleep.

Quiet,
You are an old woman,
Sleep, sleep,
Good night!

Translator: Kathleen Osgood Dana

Two Poems by Eeva Tikka

ON CHILDHOOD'S BORDER

On childhood's border I saw an angel
in the winter night
torch in hand.
It was not a question
        of a dream
        nor of childfaith
but of that which was:
        of an angel
on a snowy road

It went to the bridge and stood there
and all about it was humans' night.
Snow fell into the water and flowed
away, transformed,
and the angel's bare feet burned.
It put out the torch and looked
        at the dark like a miracle
such that is not in heaven.
Its heart was overwhelmed
        by a dream never before seen.

And slowly
it became a person.

AN ANGEL STEPS INTO THE STREAM

An angel steps into the stream
and foregoes heaven.
The water eagerly receives the angel,
out of the whirlpool bursts a
      red lily.
I see how hard it is to be human,
if your heart remembers heaven
and watery mists rise to your waist like a
      forceful caress.
I don't know what happened,
if the current got him whole
      and human
      in life and death
or would heaven call him back
asleep in the stream
on a fogbound night.

IN THE STORY'S SUN

In the story's sun
wolf fangs gleam,
the story's parents eat their children's childhood
when hunger is great.
I have not been eaten, I live
but still I fear:
A dream mussel closes and opens its shell
pearl light and dark take turns
           in a secret rhythm.

What if I were bad,
      if I ate
      my doll
      and were the wolf-stepmother
      when no one is looking?
I hide my doll.
The moon draws a new letter on the window
as if learning to read should start now.

Translators:
Kati Osgood Dana and Karen Driscoll

FINDING BIG BROTHER

by Eeva Tikka

Jorma had last been seen on the road by Rummukka's near the barn. He had exchanged several words with Sakari Havukainen, how it was a pretty morning, but not too many birds. "Didn't take your dog?" Sakari had asked, to which Jorma had replied that it didn't matter about the dog and he didn't give a darn about hunting either, just so long as he got into the woods.

But if he had taken their dog Tellu, the dog could have brought a message. Even though it was young and still barked about nothing, it would have come home and let them know something had happened. But now it was already evening and their father was out searching with the rest, but Hannu – they hadn't taken him along. He walked about, looking out the windows. The edge of the woods had been dark for a long time already.

"Didn't even take any lunch with him," his mother was saying to Saimi, their neighbor, who had stopped in for a minute. "I offered to pack him one, but he wasn't interested. And now he will be out there hungry and lost. Will they even find him before night falls?"

"He ain't lost," Hannu snapped.

They turned and looked at him: What's gotten into Hannu?

"Got a compass in his head. Said so hisself. Always knows which way to go."

"The compass must've broke," Saimi said and his mother said quietly, almost as if to herself, "Lost, that's what he is. He's lost."

"They'll find him all right," Saimi said reassuringly.

"If only it's a warm night. So long as it don't freeze."

"Don't look like that."

Hannu went outside and walked beyond the circle of light into the yard where he stood gazing into the woods. They were out there somewhere, the searchers, but they were looking in the wrong places, because they weren't finding Jorma. It was quiet, but at the same time it seemed as if the air were full of shouting.

His sister Raakel came out of the cowbarn and stood on the steps, not noticing him. In the light his face was white and odd-looking. She lingered on the steps as if she feared to go inside, and the woods sighed with shouting and silence. Jaska, Raakel's fiancé, was out there searching too.

Out toward the road, car lights cut through the low-lying fog.

Hannu lay with his eyes open so he wouldn't fall asleep until his father came. He thought how he himself would go searching tomorrow and how he would find Jorma right away. Jorma would be sitting by a campfire keeping himself warm, just as he had guessed; Jorma's leg would be broken, but otherwise he would be all right. He would be happy to see him coming; he'd been waiting for him so long.

"So you went and found me," he'd say. "The others weren't about to."

"They sure weren't," he would answer. "They didn't know how to search and looked in the wrong places. But I found you as soon as I started."

He had run and was out of breath. Jorma would notice and say, "Sit down and catch your breath."

"What about your leg?"

"It'll be all right. It don't hurt."

They sit; they aren't in any hurry and they even forget about Jorma's leg. They roast sausages over the fire, just like on a camping trip and once again Jorma tells him how he had waited and how he was certain that Hannu would be the one to find him.

When he recites this for the third time, he starts to get sleepy and falls asleep even though he didn't want to.

The smell of coffee came from the kitchen and from somewhere came the muffled yelp of a dog. Hannu sat up wondering whether he had slept too late. What had happened yesterday nudged his consciousness, but it wasn't clear at first; confusing dreams crisscrossed over and around it – and then came the clear certain knowledge: today Jorma would be found!

He threw his clothes on, listened for a moment behind the kitchen door and then opened it. There were his father and some of yesterday's searchers and some he had never seen before, one of whom was wearing a soldier's uniform and had a corporal's ribbon on his collar. They were talking quietly among themselves and didn't pay him any heed. He went to look out of the window into the yard; there were soldiers and a large, black German shepherd.

When he saw the dog and the soldiers, he was stunned; for the first time it seemed as if Jorma might really be in danger. Soldiers were needed in wars and other dangerous situations – their presence was a menace, which now affected them, which meant it affected Jorma, something bad for Jorma. But the men were standing about, peaceful enough looking; many of them were smoking. They were no different from Jorma; after all Jorma had his uniform and was in the army just like them. A week ago he had come from there, on leave – Arto at school had said something nasty about his being on leave and some girls had snickered about it too. "They don't give such long leave," Arto had said, "unless there's a special reason."

But pretty soon Jorma will probably go back. He'll put his uniform back on and will be just like them and go. Then Arto won't have anything more to say about it. Probably he's just jealous because I've got a big brother and he doesn't.

During the night it had snowed, but only lightly and it had already begun to melt in the yard. Where there was any left, it was full of the tracks of men and the dog.

"It's still spitting snow out there," his mother murmured, sounding hopeless, but no one in the kitchen said anything in reply. The men were drinking coffee and eating sandwiches and *piirakka*-pies; they didn't seem to be in any hurry and that distressed Hannu. It was almost as if everyone had forgotten Jorma, even when he had been out in the woods the whole long night. His father, even his father, was having another cup of coffee, but his fingers didn't seem capable of picking up a lump of sugar.

Then finally he rose and put his jacket on and picked up his mittens from the edge of the stove.

"Don't take those. They're still wet," his mother fretted and thrust another pair at him.

"Take care of these," his father said and went. They all went. The kitchen emptied out and Raakel opened the window so the tobacco smoke whirled out.

Hannu scooped up several sandwiches and hurriedly started to put on his outdoor clothes when his mother asked, with surprising sharpness, "And just where do you think you're going?"

"Out."

"You stay right here at home!"

Hannu pretended not to hear and put his boots on. His mother came and grabbed him by the arm and looked at him in a way that frightened him. He pulled loose from her grasp; he could still feel where she had grabbed him as he ran along the field to cut across to the road where the others were headed. Tellu had been left behind, chained up and barking excitedly; he was all riled up with the strange people and the dog coming, and jerked skittishly along his run. But Hannu, no rope held Hannu as he ran over the frozen furrows, stumbling and running and finally coming to the road.

His father glanced at him, but didn't send him away. The soldiers walked in a tight group, some smoking, the dog close by, keenly aware of its mission. The man who was holding its leash was a sergeant by the name of Sorjonen; he was much older than the recruits.

Jorma too had been a fresh recruit. Had he known those others and had they known him? He was tempted to ask, but didn't dare. The dog glanced at him indifferently. It began to sleet in big wet clumps.

"Just what we need," said Kolehmainen, swearing.

"The scent's gonna be washed out."

"Wonder if the dog'll manage to pick up the scent? What with last night's snow and all?"

"There ain't that much in the woods. And what does fall is melting as it comes.

Yep, it do appear to be meltin'. Well, boy? Hey, Kauko, did you give your boy permission to come along? We don't want to have to hunt for another one."

"Yeah, one's enough."

"Come here, Hannu," his father said. "How come Mother let you come?"

"I just left."

"So you just left, did you?" His father scrutinized him and somehow it seemed repugnant to see his eyes so close. He had been searching and had been up all night and wasn't about to believe that Hannu had come to help. "Stay with me at all times. And take care you do just that," he said.

173

After they passed the barn, they stopped. They conferred, looking at maps. In the field a flock of crows scratched at something, flinging snow and dirt about. What could it be? As they waited, Hannu went to look and the crows flew off a little distance ahead. It was a pig's foot with its hoof and hair, all muddy and dirtied. Where would they have gotten that?

Finally they left the road for the woods. He walked behind his father in the chain, and at first was excited – it would be strange if Jorma wasn't found with everything set up just for that with lots of men, soldiers, a tracking dog – the dog's presence seemed especially fine. What would Jorma say if he knew all this was on account of him?

But as the morning wore on, Hannu realized that nothing would come of it. Everything was going wrong somehow; it was as if the searchers had been led astray and even the dog stood about not knowing what to do. How could they not understand! Jorma wasn't going to be found like this!

The wet spruces creaked mockingly. They too knew better. He stopped.

"I'm going back," he told his father.

"Tired already?"

"Not tired, but..."

"If you follow that path, you'll come to the road. The other ways leads to the pond."

"Yeah, I know."

He let his father and the rest go on. He would search for Jorma alone; he had bread especially for Jorma in his pocket. He walked along the path and came pretty quickly to the road, stood there and reckoned which direction would be best to search in. They had said that the other side of the road had already been combed yesterday.

He remembered the woods with the brook. Jorma might very well have walked that far even though he had last been seen near the barn. He went after him, following the tracks that the dog hadn't noticed; along the road past the empty store, then along the tractor road into the woods, and there along the path that wound beside the brook. He knew; his legs knew; Jorma had come this way. It was as if he had the sense of smell in the soles of his feet, and each of his toes was a sensitive muzzle. He was on the trail; he had a lead the other didn't.

The new snow made the brook seem almost black. Its sound hadn't changed since summer; when he closed his eyes and listened to its babble, he could still imagine it was summer. He followed the edge of the stream; he had a goal and wasn't searching blindly like the others. This was where they had had their campfire and he knew for sure that Jorma would be there waiting for him. There they had sat in the summer and roasted sausages; Tellu had lain in the sun and they had had a tape player with them, playing softly on top of a stump. What had they talked about then? He couldn't remember, but it wasn't important. Jorma had spoken quietly and in a soft voice, and what he had said didn't stay long in your head. What had really mattered had been that Jorma had taken him along and hadn't made out that he was an awful lot bigger.

Suddenly the place they had had the fire was right in front of him. It didn't seem quite the same to him, and he paused dubiously. Then he recognized it and in the same breath denied or forgot he was expecting anything: this was the place and there wasn't anyone or anything here -- that should have been clear from the start. Its emptiness swept through and chilled him. Snow had fallen on their fireplace, the sausage sticks still stood upright between the rocks. Had Jorma set them there, or had he?

He stood there crumbling the piece of bread in his pocket. He was beginning to understand something, but when he tried to pinpoint it more exactly, it too crumbled and he couldn't put it together.

He wasn't ready to go home yet though. It was just his mother there, in that mood of hers, and Raakel. He circled the edge of the woods, catching sight of the house intermittently. He wasn't needed there or anywhere else. As he walked, he ate all the bread from his pockets, right down to the last crumbs; even so, he was a little hungry. He decided he would go home, but not quite yet.

From the swamp meadow the house could not be seen; the high, thick willows hid it. He remembered how they had made hay here in the summer; the barn was still full of the hay. He looked at the barn; all around it were magpies and crows – jumping, soaring into the air, and landing again to inspect something. Another pig's foot there? He went to see.

There Jorma lay on his face, with snow on his clothes and in his hair, hatless, his head looking odd somehow. Hannu couldn't quite comprehend – why should Jorma be here? And like this? How had it happened?

A feeling akin to hatred overwhelmed him. He wasn't supposed to have found Jorma like this. Jorma wasn't sitting at the campfire, wasn't waiting for him. He didn't need his bread. He didn't say, "Good that you came."

He just lay there. His shotgun was partially beneath him.

Hannu headed home, wetting his feet in the ditch, shoving right through the willows, and he saw the house. It looked different than it had a moment ago, and it was hard to keep going. The whole journey over the fields was difficult, and still he had to go inside and tell them.

Saimi was there with his mother and Raakel. They turned to look at him, but none of them seemed to recall that he had run out that morning. They just looked at him and waited.

"He's out there," he said. "I found him."

"Where!" shrieked his mother.

"Near the barn. He's out there. There's snow on him."

"Snow," repeated his mother despairingly; she slumped down and Saimi caught her by the arm.

"I knew it," his mother said. "I knew it, the whole fall I knew it, from the time I had that dream, the whole fall that dream has haunted me," his mother gasped, choking down her sobs.

Hannu sat on a bench, more tired than he had ever been. His hand found its way into his pocket; he remembered the bread and his hunger. But now he couldn't ask for food. He had told them. Now no one needed him any more.

The yard was filled with the tracks of soldiers, but the men had gone, as had the dog, having searched in vain for endless hours. The darkness came more slowly than it had yesterday, for now there was snow on the ground. Freezing temperatures had set in; the snow no longer melted.

Hannu bent down to pat Tellu. The dog seemed confused and looked at him inquiringly. He didn't know what had happened or maybe he did know, inside. If a person can sense something inside, as his mother had, then why not a dog?

He saw Raakel go out to accompany Jaska. They left, clasping one another tightly, without a word. After a little way, the stopped and turned toward each other, and Raakel stayed a long time in

Jaska's arms. They must be kissing, which made Hannu feel worthless and ashamed. Jaska was a year older than Jorma, had done his military service and was, in his father's opinion, the kind of man a man should be.

He wanted to yell and startle them apart, but he let them be. He didn't feel like going inside either; there they had just been talking about why no one had heard the shotgun blast even thought the barn was so close. His father had spoken, and Jaska too. But his mother had been silent. They had given her something to calm her down.

Not inside, not with them. He stood there even after Raakel had gone in; they were all there now except Jorma and him. He thought about Jorma, not about the one who had lain there in front of the barn, but the one who had sat with him and Tellu near the fire by the murmur of the brook. What had gone wrong? Why hadn't he found him there? Was it his fault? Had he searched wrong? Or had it been Jorma who had contrived to be found in such a bad, wrong way?

The thing he was striving to understand was still in crumbs at the bottom of his mind. The crumbs were hard, they scratched and hurt him, and nothing that he thought about was as it had been before. Nor was Jorma the same – the Jorma that he had roasted sausages with, who had taken him along, was still there, back in last summer. This other one, the one home on leave from the army, had gone into the woods alone and was a stranger when found.

When Hannu understood this, he felt like shouting.

Translators:
Ritva Cederström and David Colt

SOLITUDE

By Viljo Kajava

The shoreline remains in the teardrop net of evening mist
and the wave stops singing quite,
the top of a grassbound spruce sinks in the water in the
   shade.

Pale, sleepfluttered grass decks the arch of the bay,
a lone boat swims in its own shadow,
and circles, circles the songless, soundless sheep island.

Forests, dreaming, sigh on somber nights
and a leaf curls up to sleep in the shade of a leaf.
Clouds sparkle in electric dreamdown belts,
August lightning on the shore appalling in the distance:

Night and solitude, autumn coming,
I carry a black, sorrow-shiny feather
left me by a songbird.

Translators:
Steve Stone and Leo Vuosalo

Poems by Elisabet Laurila

LIKE A SONG

Like a song
Frozen in a bird's throat
by the Arctic night
Is the sigh of my blood
And the longing of my eyes
in the iron cage
of these days.

FLEEING

Farther than the froth of my days,
Farther than the sun of my nights,
Farther than my pressed lips,
Farther than your fetching eyes,
Farther than the mute carpet
of your yesterday words,
Echoes the fleeing cry of my blood.

FROM WHERE

From where do they,
These fearsome birds, come?
--the long-winged birds
That fly
Through my home's vacant panes
Into the ruin of my dream. . .
From where do these birds come?
From neither earth nor sky.
They peck my reality's tender skin
And measure the walls' depth
At the midnight moment.

DOOR

The door is open.
Let autumn
--my blood's white autumn--

Come!
The rose of fire and ashes
Lies in its bitter hand.

The strange bird of my fate
Perches behind me,
Ready to fly,
Its wings bearing
My last song's burden
--heavy, futile--
Pierced by all my dreams.

MY COUNTRY

My blue land,
My white land,
My red land:

Finland,
Borne within me
Across the world--

TRUTH

This is the truth.
This is the answer's beginning,
What must be today
And will be tomorrow.

There is still time
To choose between dreams and life,
To step beyond oneself,
To open blind eyes
And listen with both ears
To simple words,
Life's words:

Peace -- bread -- home.

TODAY

The time has come--

The forest of the masses,
The desert of people,
The happiness of the bordello,
Eros: the only god left.

You wear a servant's face
Like the stones in a wall
That seem identical.
Mass culture
Is not graven on Grecian marble
But on toilet walls.

An ocean's breadth

Translator Jill Graham Timbers

Diary Entry by Marja-Liisa Vartio

Salo January 14, 1940

My darling Diary!

It's so awfully dark I can't see anything. I am so unhappy. Every-thing feels so utterly stupid and horrid. No matter how much work I do they're never satisfied. Mom's sick and she's always nagging. Auntie's like an ogre, Unto's as horrid as -- I don't know what. In any case I feel like throwing something right in his face! Uncle Yrjö with his everlasting lectures -- just makes me want to throw up. Every place is such a mess, no matter how you try to neaten up. No one even remembers to write me a letter. I think I'll go crazy if this goes on! Tomorrow I'm supposed to go to Kommerniemi but the weather is nasty. The snow's wet and sticky, skis won't slide, roads are blocked, there's water on the ice, but I'm going, no matter what, I'll lose my mind if I can't get away from these stupid faces! I can't see anything anymore.

Kommerniemi January 20, 1940 Saturday

Dear Kauko! I cannot conceive why "mein lieber Bruder" will not condescend to write to me. No, in no way will I reprove him, I am just saying this for the opening formality. Oh darling Kake, if you only knew how much I've missed you. Especially since I'm fighting with Mom and Aunt Hilda has lied and told stories about me again. I feel so miserable and I think, if only Kake were here to talk to. Of course this stuff bores you but you mustn't mind. Right now I'm in such a dreadfully bad mood... that Aunt Hilda, to think she'd do that.

Just think, I haven't been to Luukkaala except one time since last summer, and I regret even that time. Of course it's dopey to talk about such little things now when the subject should be a bit larger fight than what's between Aunt Hilda and me... I'll quit.

Did you get my package? The second, I mean? They say there are letters for me in Salo, maybe there's a letter from you there, too?

We're sending a package now. These knee warmers, socks and bag are my crummy work. I think you'll be needing knee warmers.

I'd guess you have plenty of socks, but I'm sending these spiral socks anyway. I saw the pattern in a magazine. I think they're so neat because they don't have heels, I thought they were terrific and decided to knit you some like that. You can keep clothes in this bag, socks or whatever. I'll send you a bag later where you can keep handkerchiefs and stuff! I guess it's not so especially difficult for you there -- after all, you're not in tents at the front. It's much harder there!

Of course we'll send what you write you need. If you want some flannel underwear we can send that. And then Uncle Oski is having fur mittens made for you and Åke, the kind that have a forefinger and a thumb. From really lovely white sheepskin -- your hands sure won't freeze in these. I don't know for sure if you'll get them but they were already taken to the guy who makes them. I was just in the sauna. My hair is hanging down to the middle of my back, all wet, and my face is red and shiny as you can imagine! It's dreadfully cold here, one day it was almost 43 below. Today it was still 30 below. I was so frozen it was awful! I did exercises every night or else I would have frozen in bed.

And something else: Maikki was at the post office yesterday and she sure had a string of bad luck. She froze her nose, broke my ski, and wrote the wrong address on a letter to her boyfriend. Poor Maikki, one problem on top of another, or what would you say? We don't dare tell the mothers that Maikki broke my ski. They'd yell at Maikki did she have to go borrowing anybody's skis. Guess what we did! Maikki promised me 20 marks and she'll order and pay for a new ski to be made. We'll take the skis to a boy in Pihlajalahti tomorrow and tell him to find someone to make one. This boy has a crush on Maikki (it's not Peska) and Maikki is going to make use of it. See, Kake -- woman, woman, that treacherous creature!

The 20 marks are for me because I'll say I broke the ski myself if the mothers notice. I bet this whole tale sounds dopey to you but we don't want to tell the mothers, they'll yell at everybody even though it is just one ski! You understand!

Now I'll tell you one more funny thing. Here in Tammerniemi there's a, shall we say, lady?, named Mrs. Kyllönen. She's a little off, fights with her old man Onni till things crash. Onni thumps her on the back with a log every now and then and after every family quarrel the old lady hustles off to call Mylly-Matti (the policeman!). Mylly-Matti is on the brink of a nervous breakdown every time Esther calls and explains in a trembling voice what happened. Now this lady's Onni is at the front and of course she writes to her husband. But she doesn't know how to read or write, so Maikki serves as her scribe. Do you know what happened because Esther can't read, she by mistake put a letter she'd gotten from her husband into the envelope and sent it back to him! Just imagine the old guy's expression. I'm sure the person checking the letters wet himself laughing. Esther was hopping mad when she realized she'd sent the wrong letter. Once Maikki brought her another letter. Esther wailed and carried on, and cried in her broad Savo dialect, "If I did f-f-fight with Onni at times it wasn't anything else but l-l-love... he hit me with a log but I still l-l-love him!" Maikki says her stomach hurt from laughing so hard and you would certainly laugh too, if you could see these gentlefolk.

Yesterday the gypsies came by and of course Maikki and I had them tell our fortunes. Again the gypsy, eyes shining, hissed into my ear that I would get an inheritance. Last time she promised it all the way from America and she says I'll have three brats! Three, and I can't stand kids! Huh!

Now I have to go to sleep. But first I'm going to set my hair! Mom's going to Salo tomorrow and she'll bring my letters. I hear there are a lot!

Has Åke written you yet? Because he wrote home that he planned to write to you.

Good night, Liebling!

Gute Nacht! Marja-Liisa!

Translator: Richard Impola

THE PROCESS SERVER

By Martti Joenpolvi

1.

A woman's belt lay forgotten on the kitchen table, thin, silver-colored, only a centimeter and a half wide. Pasi knew there was a whole drawerful like them in the closet: gleaming silver and gold, black, red, and some metallic, all of them adornments, pendants rather than belts. Not a single one of them had a function like a man's belt. They were all designed and fabricated to show and emphasize a woman's hips and to rivet a man's eyes — just as his were riveted now, although the belt lay on the commonplace oilcloth of the table, to which printers' ink and a few fragments of text from a newspaper had adhered.

It seemed as if women, femininity, and the problems they caused men were made physical in the belt, which looked so vain and frivolous. Such a number of belts — women sought them as insatiably as some men sought pornography. The feeling which rose from deep within Pasi had something tender in it, and at the same time annoying merely because of that tenderness.

Marita had done a busy day's work displaying her product line, and was probably in a hotel now. Was she in her room? As alone as he was here, a man accustomed to living from a freezer? Right now there was the wrapper from a macaroni casserole among the dishes on the counter, and the stench of burned grease hung in the air of the room.

Pasi made a circuit of all the rooms and turned on the lights in every one of them. He pulled the roller shades down, and felt as if the darkness had immediately closed in more tightly around the house. The stylish furniture was all in order, the table legs bent as if the table were continually bowing to the plush, moss-green rug. And all six chairs, the humble children of the table, with thinner legs. The cupboard was of the same style, with the coffee service and wine glasses behind its glass doors, as books had once been behind the sliding glass doors of the cupboards at home. In those days he had earned his first money on his own; traveled the countryside on his bicycle one hot summer, stopping in at the slightly wealthier farms and taking orders for a book on veterinary medicine. He had sold well on his journeys, for having animals fall ill was a dairyman's nightmare. Actually he had only been selling for a book agent, and had to pay him one-half of the proceeds from the sales. His employer was a businessman in the unclear signification of the word in those days — the man preferred to stay at home and drank heavily.

This old memory from his youth came to him often now when he was at the office. He himself yearned for an agent to take care of the more unpleasant aspects of his profession. Well, actually he longed to be in the drunken old businessman's position.

Pasi smoked a cigarette on the steps outside; this had been his wife's wish when the house was thoroughly redone after the purchase. He had gone almost ten years without smoking, and then started again.

The metallic chill of the railing penetrated to his skin through his woolen shirt. The light cast by the hooded lamp conformed to the shape of its source; Pasi looked at his long shadow, which extended to the driveway leading to the main road. The ring of light did not reach quite that far; it did illuminate the side of the car. In the scant snow Pasi could see two parallel rows of footprints which emerged from the darkness into the light and onto the hard-packed surface of the yard. They had been made four days ago — it was now between Christmas and New Year, and he had taken the days off from his job as a process server.

He had wanted to save getting the tree until Kari's arrival. The boy had come on Christmas Eve, early in the afternoon. Pasi had noticed that his hair was cut oddly, clearly not the work of a professional barber. Perhaps one of Kari's fellow students had done it, perhaps it was the external symbol of some religious movement. The style reminded him of a monk. He, the father, did not ask, but he knew that the boy had joined a Friendship Service Group and went once or twice a week to visit an aged couple. The women was a wheelchair patient, and her husband did not have strength enough to push her around. Kari pushed the woman downtown, took her visiting, with her husband walking alongside. Kari had spoken of difficulties with high sidewalks, cramped elevators, steep stairs in houses without elevators where it was necessary to get the superintendent to help carry the wheelchair with the woman in it.

In the twilight Pasi had rounded up some clothes for the boy, got a pair of swampers from the garage. They had set out to get a tree from the woods nearby. Pasi had already picked one out during his autumn strolls, but it took some time to single out the spruce from among the other trees, and even then he was not sure it was the one he had picked earlier.

While sawing down the fir tree, he became aware that there was none of the feeling one usually had when getting a Christmas tree. It was no more than an occurrence in a woods with little snow on the ground: the cutting down of a fir tree. It was the same with everything: events were devoid of the feeling which once had given them individuality and context.

The boy had stood beside him, he too an oddity in his too large clothing, looking around at the trees as if at a mob. Sawdust was left lying on the snow, the stump gave off the fresh pitchy smell of spruce, and Pasi suddenly felt guilty: Trees too understand. They are filled with a mute hatred of the human species. All nature is. Even stones, in their hearts. But nature knows that atomic weapons belong to nature itself, not to man. That is natural. If man uses them, that leads to the destruction of his species, not of nature. Nature will recover: a few centuries, a few millennia perhaps, mean little to her, nature has no conception of time. Thus she is silent in the profundity of her knowledge. Perhaps she doesn't even hate? Does she pity? Or merely wonder at human folly?

On the silent return journey from the woods the thought occurred to Pasi that the development of the atomic bomb was perhaps the plan of a more profound world wisdom, intended to unsettle mankind. An omen, perhaps an opportunity given. And this was the time for people to seize the opportunity.

Kari had offered to trim the tree. As he did so, Pasi sat nearby in an armchair. He had suddenly felt a remarkable oneness with the spruce. From its needles there flowed into him the resigned sadness of the humbled piece of nature. The feeling of guilt he had felt in the woods returned, and Pasi understood that it was a common guilt that he had never been able to share — he had to feel it as his individual responsibility. In that trial, the spruce retained its individuality. None of the ribbons of tinsel, Christmas bells, or angels arranged on its boughs seemed a part of it. The tree had nothing to do with that humiliating clown costume.

188

During that Christmas dinner, Pasi recalled the first Christmas of his marriage. Actually it was the only one that stood out from the twenty Christmases that followed. They had had dinner together; Marita was expecting Kari. At the end of the meal, Marita had asked him to read the *Nativity* from their marriage Bible, which she had placed on the table that afternoon. Pasi had refused: there had been nothing Christian about his home and he had at some point even considered leaving the church. Finally Marita had demanded that he read, and when he pressed her for the reason, she had said that it had been done in her home for as long as she could remember. But Pasi had not complied with her wish and the Christmas dinner had ended with her in tears and later in a spat, which had made their first Christmas together a stormy one. Pasi had assumed that the talk of the Christmas service sprang from Marita's condition, from over-sensitivity caused by pregnancy.

There had been other stormy Christmases later. Alcohol was never the cause. Pasi came to see the cause as Marita's excessive fussing about Christmas, in which he saw something touchingly childish. And at the same time ominous: Marita fanned herself into the Yuletide spirit. And the collapse always occurred at the Christmas dinner, the high point of the evening. Marita no longer demanded that Pasi read the *Nativity*. Pasi thought Marita experience-ed Christmas as a desire for something exceptional, a supersensible way of transcending the customary. As the meal went on, his wife felt the moment she was seeking slipping out of reach, so that while they were enjoying the sliced apples preserved in a sugar sauce from the freezer, Pasi saw Marita's Christmas as being over.

This Christmas too there had been three servings of frozen sliced apples preserved in a sugar sauce waiting their turn. As Marita rose to do the dishes Pasi had gotten the Bible he had put into the bedroom and set it down near him on the corner of the table.

After they had enjoyed the cold slices of apple marinated in sugar sauce, Pasi had asked Kari to read the *Nativity*.

Now he decided to leave the car out, it would not snow tonight. A surplus of stars glittered in the sky. It was not enough to illuminate this darkness, this existing landscape the location of whose parts Pasi could fix without seeing them. The old workers' hall on the knoll, which had been restored by volunteer labor merely for sentimental reasons, beyond it the frozen open waters of the lake. Here and there small farms whose owners had dropped farming for another line of work, or practiced both at the same time. They were part-time farmers. One fairly

189

large farm, the owner of which had died recently, whose son had taken charge of the land. The son had a slew of machines: two tractors, all the new agricultural equipment, logging machinery, and a front loader. And a reaper, naturally, under the tarp at the root of a big spruce tree near the old storehouse. Pasi had gone there, chatted with the new owner, who had wondered at his knowledge of the fundamentals of agriculture.

The car stood there like a promise, newish, driven only a little over ten thousand kilometers. Once he had gotten it, except for his work travel, there was really no place to drive to. They did not have many friends, and most of their casual acquaintances lived on the other side of a brushy swamp which they did not care to cross very often. And what was a visit to them like? To sit, to notice how topics for talk shrank after the first half-hour, then discussion that limped along, until the pauses dragged out into a troublesome silence. Uncrossing one's stiffly crossed legs, hands seeking the knees and body leaning forward in a position that leads the host to assume that his guest is contemplating departure. And so the guest leaves after listening to a few polite but limp objections, thinking as he drives home that these visits are a tiresome ritual. One listens to talk with the same absent-minded devoutness as he would to the music at an organ recital. Often worthless matters are the basis for the physical nearness which is a compulsion of the human species; obligatory companionship is the social pull that congregates and disperses people, and life plays out its patterns with a monotonous dry rot, like scenes on a black and white kaleidoscope.

Pasi seldom visited his former home now, and that always during the summer. His distancing from it had begun years ago. Thinking about it later, it seemed to him that the growth of his brother's children had widened the gap. And now prospective daughters-in-law had begun to appear in the house on weekends. In Pasi's opinion they were thoroughly commonplace girls, which set him to wondering if perhaps his nephews would be dragged down by such types for the rest of their lives. As girls, all women are attractive to a degree; youth hides their doubtful points. Pasi already had the eye to see through their youth, to picture the truth after a decade or two and a few children. If a girl under twenty is tacky inside and out, a man will soon have many a dreary day to spend with her. The candidates for daughters-in-law treated him with condescension, making themselves more at home than Pasi himself did in the house where he had been born.

Suddenly his brother and nephews seemed no nearer and better known to him than anyone he met by chance on the city streets when he was on one of his unpleasant professional errands. And there was this too: Didn't every one of them know the nature of his duties? What kind of man was he. In his briefcase — it too was black — there was never anything good or agreeable. Nor was there anything such on his desk or in his mind. A process server: he knew himself now to be the bearer of all that was sad and despairing, and he could see no light up ahead. He felt himself to be on the way to an ever deeper darkness of failure. His guides on the way were the contemptuous or overtly loathing looks in people's eyes. To the wretchedness and insufficiency of the life he saw around him, he brought more ingredients for misery and despair.

What he had anticipated when he gave up his police duties had not occurred. It was true he had not had a single enjoyable day on that job either, but at his process server's task, it was as if his police experiences were internalized, and life became spiritually harder than before. Before, when carting drunks around and even on visits to homes, everything was more externalized, with the police uniform as armor in between; what he saw did not penetrate to his soul. In his new task he came to empathize more deeply with the despondency and despair that many people, his clients, endured. Shortly he became ashamed of himself and his duty, and more and more often he stated his business blushing and almost apologetically — almost as if he were the defendant.

A sturdy physique is helpful in police work. But during his years as a policeman he had been increasingly troubled by the thought that bodily size and strength were being put to a use other than those for which they were intended: farming, moving fertilizer, lifting sacks of grain. Nature had equipped him for that better than it had his brother, who with his slighter body had continued keeping up the farm.

Pasi felt his unfitness for the office work of a city dweller almost as a physical illness. In his movements there was a massive slowness, as if his frame were blindly rationing its use of energy in conformity with the seasons and their requirements. Mäkinen had even commented on it at the courthouse. His co-worker was a man who, when speaking and listening, and in the company of others, worked on his nails with a set of manicure tools always to be found in his pocket. Either he disliked looking into the eyes of others, or was indifferent or arrogant, or both.

191

In the evening solitude of the house, in his melancholy distress, Pasi picked up the woman's belt lying on the table. It weighed hardly anything, it was lighter than a single one of his thoughts about the past year — and starting a new year seemed impossible.

He felt the belt with his fingertips. It had been around Marita's waist, but the thought was not as exciting as that of holding a strange woman's belt.

Pasi thrust the end of the belt through the buckle, slipped the loop it made around his neck and pulled it taut. He loosened it only when his temples and the blood vessels in his neck were throbbing.

When the belt, now wound in a circle, lay on the table again, it resembled a strange tropical snake coiled to strike.

2.

The six o'clock plane took off. Its course as it climbed passed over the neighborhood. The process server, who had lain awake until three A. M. heard the metallic, technical howl. It was the voice of the age, like an alarm siren reminding him of the dawning day. It was the music of his daily depression.

The only restful thing left in his life was the sunlight — the same light which gives birth to all the restlessness in the world.

In the darkness of his bedroom he recalled the name of a street in a southern city: Powder Magazine Street. At one time there had actually been a red brick powder magazine on it. Walking along Powder Magazine Street as a small boy, he had wondered how people were able to live and sleep near a powder magazine.

Now he knew the answer: it was inevitable. The world itself was walking down Powder Magazine Street.

The world's oppressiveness was constantly on his mind. Perhaps God was daily present to a believer in the same way. And so were sexual exploits and fantasies to many people. A ceaseless movement from the subconscious to consciousness and vice-versa, reaching even into one's dreams.

As an adult, he had taken Powder Magazine Street to keep appointments with a doctor. He had returned from them with medications that calmed him and relieved his depression. Their only benefit was that he could think about the same horrifying things and the possibility of their occurrence more slowly and calmly, but more corrosively.

The world's tension was within him. A loose wire is more treacherous to a tight-rope-walker. He had given up on the drugs and opted for the tension.

The process server watched the egg yellows congealing, their whites bubbling. The smell of frying grease disgusted him. His wife dwelt in his mind as she dwelt in this house: as a visitor.

There was something whorish about his wife's occupation, he could not escape the thought. At this time she was waking up in a hotel room, taking a shower, putting on her makeup. She would spend the allotted hours during the early part of the day in the cosmetics section of a department store. She would be as much embellished and on display as the merchandise she was selling.

The process server reflected that people now noticed the change of seasons only through the content of magazines and the captions that proclaimed sale specials. The lack of nuance in an economy of abundance made concrete of people's minds. Getting and selling food had become just another marketplace of consumption. To the process server it seemed unnatural. The ads screamed out animal meat and organs, and behind it all there was endless killing. Life's industrial production, with death individually and by the million as its main goal.

Merely seeing a cattle truck in traffic gave the process server a chill. He thought of the animals traveling in the dismal chamber, creatures which would soon cease to be. Yet such a short time ago their eyes had glowed with the light of being.

Recently he had mentioned this to his wife. The response he got was wonderment: how could he, who had been born and brought up in the country, seen animals come into this world and leave it, a man who had seen animals butchered, not understand and accept the inevitability of it all?

The process server had said even more on that occasion. He had told of animals that had burned in their sheds through human indifference, of hundreds of thousands of animals killed by traffic, of birds caught in nets, of the massive destruction of starlings, of sea birds destroyed by oil, the brutal killing of seals' puppies for their pelts, of all the brutality practiced upon animals by human beings. Of the sufferings of laboratory animals...

And you're a part of it," he had said. You market-economy whore!"

This had not been one of those days when the process server had covertly and silently studied his wife on her return from a business trip of several days' duration, looking for a sign that would finally prove a

193

basis for the imaginings that troubled him, a sign that would confirm the rightness of his decision. He had followed his wife's actions as she made ready for her demonstration trips; she no longer decked herself out for him. The process server understood that he was an article of bedroom furniture — a full-length mirror whose duty it was to nod when a certain degree of preparedness had been achieved.

He could see that his wife's features had taken on a certain harshness brought on by layered cosmetics. In her voice there was sometimes a strained overtone, like a nasty blade, ready to slash and belittle her husband's ideas. She was prone to gibes and repartee which he regarded as malicious.

He thought of his wife and her sisters — these three women — and of their similarities. They had all adopted belittling attitude toward their husbands. That fact these women, who had grown closer with age, were quite willing to make public: Oh, he can't..." Somehow it came out as if they were saying, But other men can..." He had noticed his mother-in-law's features becoming dominant in them, shaping them individually in the way that a final version of a sketch develops or an embryo in a womb takes on details one by one.

When day had more fully dawned, up amidst the clutter of discarded objects in the cold attic, the process server reached into the dark recess under the eaves. With a bundle of magazines now under his arm, he returned to the kitchen in the gray light of the December day, found some matches, and went down to the basement sauna.

There he sat on a stool in front of the firebox and undid the dusty bundle. It contained a number of publications it was time for him to get rid of. They had come into his hands after a police raid on a certain tobacco shop.

He lighted a small pile of birch bark on the grate and fed in the sheets one by one. They were of good quality glossy paper, with sharply defined color prints.

The process server watched the paper women burning, watched their nippled breasts disappear, saw their pubic hairs singed, their labia shriveling up before burning. Their rounded bellies, their feminine navels, the fullness of their buttocks ceased to exist. He saw their faces burn, some of them so familiar to him in a way that he sometimes imagined having spotted them among crowds in the street. They were more real to him than many of the faces of women he had known in the flesh.

It took longer than he had expected. The paper, weighted by dampness, was hard to burn. The process server had to build up the fire.

After an hour he returned to the sauna. Some of the pages had charred in such a way that the form of the living women on them had survived as a negative. He poked among the ashes, and as he scooped them up into a pail, he made sure that no traces of the women remained.

The process server carried the ashes to a compost cage he had built in the back yard. It had begun to snow.

The process server recalled a certain harvest time, August evenings when his wife had been juicing currants. He saw her carrying the pulp of the fruit to the compost late at night, her shape fading into the incipient August darkness. Moths swarmed around the yard lamp and the spruce trees bore silence high on their tops. He had felt a deep sadness for the end of summer and old memories that were no longer very real.

He had seen red juice stains on the kitchen floor and had needed to hold on to the edge of the table for support.

3.

It snowed all that afternoon, evening, and night, and was still snowing on the following day, New Year's Eve.

Pasi had opened a path to the road. Marita parked the company's car in front of the light winter garage placed halfway up the driveway. She saw Pasi shoveling snow off the cement steps going down to the side door which led to the baking room.

The baking room, and especially its genuine farm baking oven, had attracted Pasi when they had come to check the house with the intention of buying it. At some time during the fifties, the builder of the house had done cobbling there as a sideline. When he sold the house he was already an old man, and the smell of leather had already vanished from the baking room transformed into a shoemaker's shop.

Marita was astonished: Pasi had never before shoveled snow away from the side door. It had been allowed to pile up there; for the door was never used and might not even have opened properly.

He's doing it for his health, Marita thought.

The purchase of the house had been Pasi's desire and his decision. He had liked just this place. It was in the country, but close to the city: a recent annexation had made it part of the city. There were advantages to that: municipal technology was being developed here, houses had been newly constructed and others begun. This was no dying neighborhood which people were abandoning. Its center — the school, bank, postoffice, a couple of grocery stores — were a half-kilometer away. It had up-to-date street lamps that shone in the sky beyond the woods to the west.

How different everything was now from in the spring, when Pasi had spent the bright hours of the night alone on the porch. His odd vigils had sometimes lasted until well into the morning. When Marita went to see, she would find that Pasi had gone off; the empty woven chair creaked to itself as the just-risen sun dried the remnant of the night's dew from it.

During spring planting Pasi had wandered alone checking the sprouting fields of winter grain, watched the farm machinery at work in the fields, plowing and tilling and planting. All summer long he had followed the growth of the crops and told Marita of all its phases as if he owned all the tilled fields in the area. And sometimes when he had a vacation at hay- making time, he had helped the aging couple nearby, who were hard pressed to keep up with the work on their dairy farm.

Pasi had been enthusiastic about a home garden, had planted berry bushes and started a vegetable patch. From windows left over when the house was renovated, he built a greenhouse. He grew lettuce and tomatoes. The air in the porch, warmed by the spring sun, was thick with the scent of earth from the tomato plants. Pasi practiced organic gardening. His neighbor provided him with cow manure in exchange for help with the hay- making.

It had been that way.

Last summer Pasi had not taken part in hay-making. He had not planted tomatoes. When Marita asked why, he said he was letting the land rest.

Marita could date the start of the change quite accurately. In April, when the snow cover was thin, Pasi began the early spraying of the orchard. Marita saw that for the first time the task was repugnant to him, he was stirring the carbolic solution so listlessly. The piston in the spray pump broke almost immediately, and the work was left unfinished. Pasi did not repair the sprayer, although all it needed was new packing for the piston. The bucketful of solution disappeared somewhere; it could still be smelled near the back of the lot at the end of May before heavier rains came.

Exhausted by the long drive, Marita looked out the window at the snow-bright yard. Her shopping bag sat unemptied on a chair. It was heavy because along with the rest it contained two bottles of wine. It seemed to her that along with the sprayer, something within Pasi had broken during those dead days of April. She would like to have repaired the place, gotten the man to function again, up from the gloom and silence into which he had sunk during the summer and autumn after his wakeful spring. She had even begun to think that the move here had been a mistake after all.

Marita saw Pasi plodding through the snow carrying an aluminum dish with oats in it, and remembered his wondering why the female pheasant was outwardly so much plainer than the male.

The pheasant species had multiplied rapidly in the wooded hollow crossed by a meter-wide winding brook. Pheasants moved about the yard, and they guessed that the birds were spending the night under the spruce tree there. Marita remembered well the time they had guessed at it. They had been standing side by side near the spruce, and Marita had been reminded of their wedding. The spruce tree stood there like the preacher, and Marita was on the verge of saying: I do. It was this that made her remember; it was a moment of life after so much had died.

It was a quite symmetrical spruce tree, whose thick trunk branches went right down to the ground and made a good shelter for the birds. Pasi was in the habit of buying sacks of oats and sprinkling the grain on the snow near the spruce.

Once Pasi had come in with two pheasant tail feathers in his hand. He had found them on the roadside and supposed that little boys had pulled them from the bird on their way to school. There was congealed blood on their quills. And there were tears in Pasi's eyes.

He had become so soft-hearted.

Pasi had started studying books on parapsychology and had recently talked about the possibility of rebirth.

A little before midnight on New Year's Eve, Pasi hung some sparklers on the tree. He had found them in a cardboard box in the woodshed. They were old, dating all the way back to their son's childhood, even the outside of the case looked old. The box in his hand was like testimony to the abrupt ending of Kari's childhood. Pasi felt as if, like the unused sparklers, he had omitted giving something to his son. It was a vague remnant in his mind, he did not know what to do with it, it was doubtful if he could any longer bring it forth whole and fit for use.

197

He had found the sparklers in a shoe box where Christmas-tree trimmings were kept. The box itself was like the trimmings, a Christmas heritage. In Pasi's opinion ornaments should be kept for the year in just this environment, a faded cardboard box. On the days leading to Christmas, Marita had often suggested that they get new trimmings. Pasi did not want them, so that year after year the tree was modest and old-fashioned. And if at Marita's doing a new ornament appeared, Pasi hung it last on the tree and viewed it as a thing apart from the familiar trimmings. In them Pasi felt something of the Christmas that was no longer accessible.

The old sparklers burned well. Pasi watched their flashing in the room soberly and devoutly. He picked up their scorched hulls from the branches and while he was thoughtfully bending their wire cores, there was a loud bang somewhere.

Marita raised a shade in the kitchen and peered out the window to see the fireworks. There was nothing to be seen, and nothing further was heard. Just a single bang.

When she returned to the living room with a full wine bottle in her hand Pasi was no longer there.

He was lying naked from the waist up on the bed in the dark bedroom. His face was pressed into a pillow and his hands were gripping its corners.

Marita sat near him on the side of the bed, lowered a hand to his shoulders, and felt their twitching. His fingers were jerking, his whole body shaking, and Marita knew that he was fighting against a violent crying jag.

It was incredible in such a strong man.

Marita was silent. After he calmed down, Pasi said:

"It's so hard..."

Marita searched for words, found them. While speaking she stroked her husband's back and shoulders as if she were spreading an ointment on his skin to alleviate her words.

The new year had arrived.

4.

Marita awoke to the shriek of a pheasant. She reached out an arm to feel. Pasi's place in the bed was empty.

A thin sliver of light from the open sliding door shown on the white carpet revealing nap flattened by footsteps. On this the first Monday of the new year, Pasi had risen in the earliest hours of the morning.

There were two more shrieks from the pheasant and the sound of shaking, although one could not really tell for sure if the bird were actually shaking itself or if the aural effect was somehow related to the bird's cry.

The front door opened. Marita got up from the bed. There was a half-dried saliva stain on Pasi's pillow.

Pasi was leafing through a newspaper he had fetched from the mailbox at the roadside. Marita could feel the cold outside air his jacket gave off through her nightgown.

Pasi was not reading. He was not even wearing his glasses. He turned the pages nervously as if looking for a particular news item. When Marita asked why he was up so early he said he wanted to check something on the car before leaving.

Marita saw him go into the foyer and from there to the basement stairs. She could hear the receding sound of his descending footsteps. The newspaper was left open on the table.

The basement of the house was low and there was always a stagnant earth-smell there because of poor ventilation. A door led to the garage from it so that one did not have to go outside.

The process server did not use that door. He looked at the meter on the central-heating boiler, looked into the dim recess where the oil tank was, then opened the door beside it and stepped into the baking room.

He turned on the light and saw the snow he had shoveled from the steps pressing against the outer pane of the diamond-shaped basement window. He took off his jacket and opened the buckle of his belt.

He opened the door of the baking oven, felt for an object in the darkness, and enclosed it in his large, grasping, farmer's hand.

The process server knelt down beside the baking oven, put the pistol into his mouth, set it at an angle to the hard palate, and shot himself.

Translator: Seija Paddon

Poems by Juice Leskinen

I would like to dedicate the following translations to my Tutorial Group
1995-1996, Department of English, University of Helsinki.

GENESIS

(i)

In the beginning god created heaven and earth.
That was the beginning of man's
creative work:
in the beginning he created God who created
heaven and earth.

(ii)

He made himself into a nest for his God.
For the Devil he created a conference hotel:
five stars for language skills at the check-in,
free parking and service.

(iii)

The earth was barren and empty.
Man reads the Bible
backwards from cover to cover,
from comma to comma;
he makes crosses of dashes by cancelling them,
overlooking them.
What will become of him when it's the end of man
the earth is barren and empty?

(iv)

(up to this point things have happened here & elsewhere si-
multaneously;)

Planets, galaxies, universes
stir man in his head.
    As far as he is concerned, it is
    a black reality without an opening, the likeness of
brains,
only bigger, even bigger yet.
    In the hundred percent class.

THE FIRST STAGE

INDEPENDENCE DAY 1939

The Russians came in November,
in December, leave-taking.

Ma left Finland for Finland,
      from East to West the way Finland has always moved
      on the wing of the Sun

Ma left, she had to
      when Stalin's organ played Säkkijärvi polka
      all to hell

As a child, Ma called a Russian a Russian
      as a young woman she had to learn to say
      (Ru)sshh!(n),
now, wiser by decades, she dares to say
it doesn't pay
      to fry a Russian in butter, even.

SUCH A LIFE, MA

Such a life, Ma,
 one could write a play about it,

but if one wrote it, it'd be
impossible to act, impossible to stage

nobody would watch it
nor would there be a critic who'd believe it, not voluntarily

Ma, it's such a life
 one has to live it
 for it to be real

THE DEAD, FIRST SERIES

First she buried her brother:

made her brother, my uncle, the deceased uncle,
    that was a natural death,
    the war walked towards and over him.

Then Ma buried her mother;
    she was killed by cancer and sorrow,
    the Finnish twin powers,
    and peace, since one no longer had to stay
    awake, then.

I never met this Granny;
    the killers move among us still.

THE DEAD, SECOND SERIES

The town doctor killed your first-born daughter.
Ma buried the child, embarrassed:
    this is not what's supposed to happen;
    Nature not following her own rules!

Then was born a boy;
he is writing his Ma into these stanzas

Then was born a boy, water-on-the-brain, died and was
                                  buried.
Then was born a boy who lived half a year, died and was
                                  buried.

Then was born a boy,
    stubbornly, he grew all the way up to Master of Arts.
    Sometimes he goes to work wearing a tie
    and is allowed to express his opinion.

We've been busy at giving birth,
    hard at dying,
    and real devils at living.

DOCTORS

They know,
and it's known.

They're too clever for human beings;
    they possess all the present knowledge,
    they've walked the map to its edge,
but the terrain continues past the paper.

They're high and mighty, all of them
        and Mengeles the rest:

the greatest advances lie in finding a label for the causes of
death
        through which uncertainty oozes
        the way it does from human hands

VIRGIN BAY IN A DREAM

I've only gone there in a dream.
Only in a dream is it real.

> JSP in the foundation stone of a house left standing
> after a fire, horizontal line inward from the door-opening,
> from another, a vertical one,
> > albeit limping, into civilian ranks

Bodies, body fragments, eyes drained empty,
the under twenty-year-olds' arms made useless
in crushed shoulders....
at these parties death is an invited guest,
life zeroed,
"halt"-light burns by smouldering

Only the "lottas", doctors and tortured military material.
There are those who escaped this dream: Pentti Saarikoski (still a
    child),
Taina Elg (a precocious youth), Cyril Szalkiewicz and Ma

A functionary arrives: impeccable dress and clean hands
He says:
    - I do have a good position, yes sireeee...

MOTHER TONGUE RECONSIDERED

Ma came from Karelia to Savo
I came from Savo to Häme
   I have never spoken my mother's tongue.

DEAR MONSTER-BRAT

Ma says that she couldn't keep me
in a stroller, even, as a kid:
     I would roll over on to the ground and
     run to fetch flowers for Ma

And I wasn't put in a harness,
     even those who didn't want to relinquish their own
     couldn't harness me

A girl cousin tied me to a tree and forgot me;
     I didn't get upset, but the cousin still remembers
        her rope;
I suppose we're both tied to it still

THE FIRST BIKE

To the boy it seemed so big
it couldn't be just one person's means of transportation.

And it wasn't,
        it had been in the war;
        with it Finland had been pedalled on her way again.

I kept blowing at many bruises
thinking
        there have been others falling off this bike before.

THE OSTENSIBLE PHILOSOPHERS

Life, like an onion,
    they say, these provincial philosophers
    whose greatest dream is a line in the *Readers
Digest*,

has to be peeled layer by layer
sliced, ground,
    and enjoyed
    although at times it makes you cry.

Shall I tell them, emphasize, that life,
    like an onion, has to be
    handled with a sharp knife,
    without hesitation.

It makes you cry, just the same.

THE FIRST AXE

Granny, my father's mother,
gave me an axe when I was six.

I can still remember - or imagine, the same thing -
how according to her logic she arrived at that:
since grandfather was a carpenter and the boy six,
there was an obvious need for an axe.....

I'll give my son an axe
        will tell him that not a single log cabin family
        has been driven with it out into snow

        nor will be driven
        since that's what Ma says.

EVERYDAY WORLD POLITICS

So many want to wake us up with hate,
so many love us to death.

Translator: Seija Paddon

MIRROR

By Jyrki Kalliokoski

MIRROR
I need contact, tac-tac-o-tac-contact
(Peter Gabriel)

I carried the mirror all through the city. I had asked the salesman not to wrap it in paper although I hadn't yet realized what-all the mirror could show me. At the Hakaniemi market, a drunk took a salt herring out from its wax paper wrappings, stuffed the fish into his mouth, grimaced and then for some reason spat it out onto the sidewalk. This was something I needn't have watched. I saw it in the mirror which happened to be at the same height as the man who was bending down in an odd position. I realized other things would also be shown to me in a similar fashion, things I wouldn't have the nerve to meet with my own eyes. It would no longer be necessary for me to stare at the world. I had a receiver, a mirror I could look at. And even if I didn't look at it, the mirror would receive all the images the world offered.

I carried the mirror all through the city. Actually, without even thinking what-all the mirror could show me, I had asked the salesman in the store not to wrap it in paper. Sales people were putting the wares of their market stalls back into boxes; tomatoes and cucumbers, lettuce and squash, carrots and turnips disappeared back into vans; I saw it all while hurrying with the mirror under my arm out of the store and across the market place to a streetcar stop.

From the very first moment the mirror led me. It possessed me and imprisoned my eyes. When I carried it, tilted upward under my left arm,

213

it projected city scenes to me which changed at the speed I moved; the otherwise familiar city scenes were now altogether new and different. The people, the market place, cars, familiar streets were, when reflected from the surface of the mirror into my eyes, part of some new, framed picture, reality which the mirror encased and imprisoned. A person in the market place or a car in the street were not, after all, a person in the market place or a car in the street, but a person in the picture the mirror (30 x 120 cm) reflected, which reflected a person in the market or a car was a car in a picture which reflected a street full of cars.

I had, of course, always understood that the reality I thought I saw was only my projection of some reality in a way I thought I was seeing it. Now as my eyes were prisoners of the mirror, naturally I couldn't believe that those endlessly changing 30 x 120 cm pictures were *Reality*. Of course I understood that they were (at that exact moment) a series of projections of reality, one projection endlessly following another as they do in a film, but - on the other hand - I couldn't help but be fascinated by the thought that they might be *Reality.* At the very least they could be as real as that which I had, for all my life, considered to be reality - in latter years against my better philosophical judgment - as real as the projections absorbed into my mind while seeing them, or at least as I thought I saw them.

With the mirror in my lap, and while watching these pictures as I sat in a street car, I began to think up a story about someone who would search for his life in the surface of a mirror, would project as his reality only that which the mirror happened to catch within its frame. That kind of a story could begin like this:

Pekka carried the mirror all through the city. He had asked that the salesman not wrap it in paper although he barely sensed yet what-all it and innumerable other mirrors might show him.

All his life Pekka had had to hear that he stared at his reflection much too often in all kinds of windows. While sitting in a bus, he switched from looking at houses, people, and parks speeding by to examining his own face which the bus window carried forward the way the changing houses, people, and parks were speeding by in the background. The darker it got outside, the more difficult it was to distinguish houses, people, or parks while his own face became all the more distinct in the bus window. At times an odd feeling surprised him, brought on by the way a passenger on the bus would notice his "mirroring", perhaps laugh or otherwise show contempt for a person who

214

kept examining his own face - or at least the passenger would let him know it looked funny.

The city, however, was full of traps: store windows, glass doors, gleaming chrome surfaces, steel and copper, recently washed car bodies, transparent plastic screens confronting those who lined up in front of a cafeteria cashier. One quick look was enough, one penetrating look at whatever happened to be the scene that turned one's thoughts to one's face. For years Pekka had pondered his relationship with life and other people. So often it felt like one's entire life was actually made up of accomplishing things or of performances. A visit to a store or a library, sitting in a café or walking along a street was a performance, not to mention an evening in a theatre or a rock club. As if people truly expected some sort of an achievement, something that had to be realized there and then. In reality, it could also be that people were so focused on how to get through their own performances that they were incapable of evaluating the performance of others except by happen-stance, and a little at a time. But what if during those precise few moments of actual control one failed. It is, after all, based on these accomplishments that one is judged. That is why one had to be continuously conscious of the level of one's performance.

Was the search for the image of one's own face in transparent, reflective surfaces really that self-conscious? Probably not. It was difficult to stop looking through surfaces and layers of other images reflected in those surfaces at one's own face which could be constantly changing and showing a gay, sad, worried, perky, friendly, or aloof expression, and each expression could be endlessly examined and further changed. These expressions could be examined from the point of view of their genuineness, ability to convince, degree of success, and the depth of their expressed emotional state or attitude.

Sometimes a person searching for his face in a mirror can meet the eyes of another. When that happens, usually both turn their eyes away, embarrassed. The most painful situation happens during fittings in stores where you have one mirror for three fitting rooms and one has to compete with another customer from another booth for the reflective surface and this in front of other customers and an impatient sales clerk.

Pekka was not looking for his own face in the mirror. Examining the outside world in the surface of mirrors turned out to be more fascinating. He found that it wasn't necessary to stare directly and arrogantly at people and events, but it was possible to observe reality more subtly with the aid

of a reflective surface. On the one hand, this curtailed possibilities for observation; on the other, it made it possible to choose reality over chaos, the most appropriate part from the stream of visual information, one sectioned by the mirror's frame or the edges of some other shining surface. Besides, usually there were several shining surfaces in the same situation so that whoever was examining the world in them was not limited to only one mirror.

It was strange that when buying the mirror for his hallway he didn't remember at all his passion for "mirroring" himself. His thinking about the hallway mirror was, at least on the conscious level, merely a matter of interior decoration, though he had reasoned, of course, it would be good to see how he looked when he left for work. Only when he was on his way home and while, as if instinctively, he followed what was moving on the street, he began to understand the possibilities offered by the mirror he carried. He had time to be frightened of the speed of his thoughts; like a spy, he could walk along familiar streets and look at everything from an entirely new perspective.

The girl (or woman) looked straight at him. That is what he thought at first. But the woman looked straight into the mirror, smiled at him in his mirror. Had she smiled like that for some time already, Pekka didn't know. In his confusion he changed the position of the mirror slightly, and the woman disappeared from his sight. But she didn't disappear from the streetcar where Pekka sat. The woman was two seats away, and Pekka knew that. He tried to guess whether or not she was still smiling and how? Was it with surprise, amusement or still with the same mysterious friendliness as in the mirror, except now Pekka had ended that smile in his Reflected Reality. In Actual Reality, the woman could conceivably still be smiling, but would Pekka want to look at this reality with his own eyes, or would he dare merely to turn the mirror back to the same position and look for the woman's smile in it. The streetcar stopped. When it moved again, Pekka could no longer see the woman in his mirror. She had gotten off at the Convention Hall stop. Pekka turned the mirror so that he could look at the feet of passengers walking forward in the isle.

Of course the look the woman had given him continued to bother him. It was very unlikely that they would ever meet again. (That their eyes had met was what had happened.) But the same kind of situation might happen again. Actually it was quite plausible that the same kind of situation would confront him again some day, perhaps in some other streetcar, bus, park, or kiosk. The woman had been beautiful. Her smile wise, understanding and somehow calming despite the sensual nature of the situation. And again he noticed how lackadaisical his thoughts were: the image of the woman in the mirror had been beautiful, her smile in that picture had pleased him. But now she was no longer there, nor was her image. The only one Pekka could keep, and the one which he would have to try to preserve, was the picture in his mind of a mirror-image of a beautiful woman's look and smile, a woman who had travelled in the same streetcar with him. He understood now the difference between a picture and a mirror- image; the mirror image is doomed to disappear, the world is on the move as is the mirror; what was on the surface of the mirror a moment ago is no longer there. Of course one could lose a picture or tear it up, and it would be the same as losing one's mirror or breaking it. But when the world changes and the mirror moves on, the beautiful picture on the surface of the mirror disappears for all time. The mirror doesn't empty itself, but no one can guarantee that it will ever again reflect anything as interesting. (Pekka didn't want to look at people's shoes, but felt that he didn't have the strength to meet another person's look right away, not in the mirror, or directly either, for that matter. Best to close one's eyes for the remainder of the trip.)

It was eleven o'clock one evening when Pekka was in a restaurant leaning against the bar. At the end of the day's work which had stretched very late, he only wanted to have a bottle of beer and then go home. He stared at the rows of glasses and different bottles behind the bar. There wasn't much to look at. The female bartender had disappeared somewhere behind the rows of glasses and bottles. However, it was difficult to turn around and start staring at the dining room. Then he remembered his pocket mirror. He took it out of his breast pocket and began cautiously to scan the guests in the restaurant. The place was almost empty. At the side tables, at the edges of the room and far from the bar, sat single guests or couples. There were no groups. It was so quiet there it actually made you sleepy. Pekka played with his mirror, moving it at the level of his elbows which were resting on the bar, and he took careful glances at it. By moving one's wrists suitably fast, you got a kaleidoscope-like sense: the sleepy and ordinary restaurant dining room was going around and around as a mixture of colours, lights, and shapes. In the middle of this he drank his beer, barely looking at his glass, enjoying his kaleidoscope game.

Sometimes it takes a long while before we realize that someone is staring at us. Pekka was so engrossed at observing the shifting pictures on the surface of his pocket mirror he didn't notice right away that he, himself, was the focus of observation. Suddenly he raised his eyes from the level of his elbows and faced the gaze of a woman in front of him, the same woman whose smile he had imprisoned in his mirror while they were riding on the street car.

Was everything a matter of mere chance? Was this merely a chance happening? The same smile which again caught him playing with a mirror, caught him off guard and yet, reassured him. The same woman stood in front of him now. Again he found himself not thinking clearly; after all, he was looking straight at a large mirror behind the bar. (How had he not seen it but rather been satisfied to play with his small pocket-mirror?)

Now he had to behave properly. A restaurant bar was, after all, an altogether different place for meeting someone's eyes than the Mannerheim Way streetcar. If the woman's eyes were in the same large mirror as his, she must be sitting at the same bar, beside him. To the left or to the right? To the left? It was difficult to concentrate. Pekka felt his heart pounding.

It wasn't as if he needed to look to either side. Neither did the woman. After all, she was looking into the mirror. He had to look into the same mirror. You couldn't move the mirror, it remained out of reach for them both where they were, at the other side of the bar. Everything depended on their movements, their glances. That bar mirror was like an opening, a bridge or a street crossing, an agreed-upon meeting place. It was a permanence which existed and remained, and in which they had to meet each other.

The bartender came and asked Pekka if he wanted another beer. Pekka nodded but didn't take his eyes off the mirror and the woman. The woman was watching him while he paid for his beer, following his every movement. Pekka felt her looking at him, observing him take out his wallet, looking at the bills he paid with, and whether or not he left a tip. Of course he didn't leave a tip but collected all the twenty, ten, and fivepenny coins from the bar and dropped them into the wallet he had taken out again. You couldn't judge from the woman's looks what she thought of his behaviour. Nevertheless, Pekka felt he was being judged. That was a very awkward feeling. After his beer was placed in front of him, he didn't know what to do next. For a moment he dropped his eyes to the glass, but didn't take a sip. Then he made a mistake. He felt his courage betray him. He decided to go to the men's room. There he washed his face with cold water, ran the fingers of his both hands through his hair and returned to the bar, but the woman had disappeared. Because of his indecision he had lost her for the second time.

After finishing his beer, Pekka felt it hadn't been the last time he would see the woman in the mirror, but he had no idea how quickly after this events would follow one another and what he still would see and experience before it all came to an end.

In the Taxation Centre Pekka was directed to the second story offices. After explaining his errand to one official, he was led to another. This one listened to Pekka without interrupting him but with a look of disinterest. When Pekka had finished, the official told him he needn't worry. The problem about which Pekka had come didn't actually concern him as long as his yearly income didn't exceed 150,000 marks. Annoyed, yet relieved, Pekka walked down the stairs and stepped out onto windy Merihaka street. At the Hakaniemi market he went into a café. Bent over his cup of coffee he looked out the window toward the market. On the street in front of the café a couple was kissing. When the man's head moved away from blocking the woman's face, Pekka realized he was staring at the woman he had seen in the restaurant yesterday, the woman who now with her eyes closed was kissing another man. Pekka wanted to turn his head away, but his eyes were fixed on her and on the strange man while they were sucking at each other's lips. People were walking between Pekka's window and the kissing pair, but Pekka didn't turn his head.

The woman slapped the man's face and rushed into the café, to the table next to Pekka's without noticing him, or so it seemed. There was no mirror anywhere near. He was forced to meet the woman face to face. And they had to speak.

In the woman's bedroom, high above her bed, there, in the ceiling, was a large mirror with a wooden frame. As he lay down on his back, Pekka looked for a moment at the reflection of himself naked. Then he turned to watch the woman who was just then removing her panties. He looked at her, her breasts, took hold of her hands and drew her over him.

The woman had asked if he didn't think it odd that they met so often in different places. And, Pekka had added, that they always found themselves in different mirrors. But not this time, now here we are,

219

face to face at the same table, and there are no shining surfaces between us, only air, the woman had said. And we can even touch each
other, Pekka had said and surprised himself with his bravery when he
had reached out to smooth her hair. The woman had smiled and looked
at him eye to eye with a kind of penetrating friendliness, and after that
she took Pekka's free hand. I can't take the streetcar home alone today. I want us to walk, eyes closed, hand in hand, home along the
Töölöbay shore, she had said. Pekka had stopped stroking her hair,
bent over the table, kissed her very quickly so that she didn't actually
have time to respond. Afterwards, a few falling raindrops had made
rings on the surface of the bay, but they hadn't noticed them because
they had tried to walk from Hakaniemi to Töölö with their eyes closed.

In answering with his body the woman's movements while lying on
his back, Pekka kept his eyes closed in enjoyment, and caressed her
breasts with his hands. In the middle of the swaying movement he remembered the mirror in the ceiling. He opened his eyes and watched
his breathless face and the woman's moving back, legs, and bottom in
the surface of the mirror. It reflected the expression of their enjoyment
exactly. The more he looked at his face and the faceless woman over
him, the better he felt. With his body he felt the movement of her body
against his own, with his eyes he saw the movement he felt, and he
could read his feelings in the reflection of his face.

In the mirror the image of the lovers' movements and their bed was
clear and distinct. The mirror reflected every movement of the bodies in
precise detail, imprinted every enjoyment on Pekka's face. Even at the
moment of climax, Pekka kept his eyes open and looked up to the ceiling. And as the big mirror fell, he still had time to realize how the ex-
actness of the picture clouded up and disappeared before he was
crushed under the woman and his heavy mirror image.

It was amazing, actually, that the camera had stayed in such good
shape despite the fall. I took the film out, first thing, put it in its con-
tainer and stored it with the other films. In the morning I watched it
from the beginning to the end. Behind the mirror, it had preserved
Pekka's expressions, his last expression immediately preceding the dis-
covery. Perhaps it was good that things happened the way they did. I
had already grown tired of looking for places to hide the cameras. I had
thought Pekka innocent right from the beginning. Now it didn't matter,
and I no longer had to insist on that to my employer. He could look
through all the films once more. As I was on my way out, I straight-

ened the hair on my forehead and felt the growth of beard on my cheeks while I glanced in the mirror in the office hallway.

Bibliography of Translated Texts

1. **WHAT IS THE OLD ONE TO DO?** From Fredrika Runeberg: *Teckningar och drömmar* [Drawings and Dreams], 1861.

2. **ON CHILDHOOD'S BORDER** and Other Poems by Eeva Tikka. From Eeva Tikka: *Enkeli astuu virtaan.* [an Angel steps into the stream]. Jyväskylä 1991.

3. **"FINDING BIG BROTHER"**. From Eeva Tikka: *Alumiinikihlat*. [Aluminum engagement rings]. Jyväskylä. 1993.

4. **SOLITUDE**. From Viljo Kajava: *Tuuli, valo, meri. Runoja vuosilta 1935-1982*. [The Wind, Light and the Sea. Poems from 1935-1982]

5. **LIKE A SONG** and Other Poems by Elisabet Laurila. From Elisabet Laurila: *Elisabethin runoja* [Elisabeth's Poems].n.d.

6. **DIARY ENTRY** by Marja-Liisa Vartio. From Marja-Liisa Vartio *Ja Sodan Vuosiin Sattui Nuoruus* [And Her Youth Fell During the War Years]. (Journals and letters) Art House 1994.

7. **"THE PROCESS SERVER"**. From Martti Joenpelto: *Haastemies* [The Process Server]. 1984.

8. **GENESIS** and Other Poems by Juice Leskinen. From Juice Leskinen: *Äeti*. Runoja [Mother. Poems]. Helsinki: Kirjayhtymä, 1994.

9. **"MIRROR"**. From Jyrki Kalliokoski: *Peili ja parta* [Mirror and Beard]. Helsinki: WSOY, 1991.

Contributors to *Connecting Souls*

Kaarina Brooks, poet and translator, lives in Alliston, Ontario

Mary Caraker, author, lives in San Francisco, California

Ritva Cederström, translator, lives in Binghamton, New York

Kathleen Osgood Dana translator and author, lives in Northfield, Vermont

Karen Driscoll, writer and translator, lives in Portland, Maine

Paula Erkkila, poet and writer, lives in Berkeley, California

Marlene Ekola Gerberick, poet and visual artist, lives in Bath, Maine

Harry Gustafsson, poet, lives in Brampton, Ontario

Ernest Hekkanen, writer and poet, lives in Vancouver, British Columbia

Lisa V. Heverin-Davis, writer, lives in North East, Maryland

Eija I. Heward, writer, lives in Duxbury, Massachusetts

Bernhard Hillila, poet and writer, lives in Valparaiso, Indiana

Ted Jansen, writer, lives in Toronto, Ontario

Diane Jarvenpa, poet, singer and composer, a.k.a. Diane Jarvi, lives in Minneapolis, Minnesota

Pentti Junni, poet, lives in Thunder Bay, Ontario

Helen Koski, poet, lives in Toronto, Ontario

Lynn Maria Laitala, writer and editor, lives in Bennett, Wisconsin

Mark B. Lapping, poet, lives in Portland, Maine

Lorraine Kasari Loiselle, poet, lives in Pittsburgh, Pennsylvania

Mikko Mallinick, poet, lives in Toronto, Ontario

Seija Paddon, translator, lives in Keswick, Ontario

Jane Piirto, poet and writer, lives in Ashland, Ohio

Erika Pollari, poet, lives in Toronto, Ontario

Burt Rairamo, poet and writer, lives in Toronto Ontario

Carol Ruotsala Staats, poet, lives in Wasilla, Alaska

Steve Stone, translator, lives in Mayhill, New Mexico

Jill Graham Timbers, translator, lives in Normal, Illinois

Börje Vähämäki, translator, lives in Beaverton, Ontario

Susan Vickberg-Friend, poet and visual artist, lives in Toronto, Ontario

Leo Vuosalo, translator, lives in Helsinki, Finland